mumhood

how to handle it

why it matters

Ross Mountney

Dedication and Thanks

Dedicated to all the wonderful mums out there.

And in special appreciation of all those dearest mum friends
who shared the mumhood journey with me, listened
to my ramblings and contributed their own.

Enormous thanks also to those who helped
me prepare and publish this book.

And in loving acknowledgement of my beautiful children
without whom I wouldn't have grown into who I am now!

About the author

Ross is a passionate mum and writer who, although delighted by motherhood, spent much of it thinking 'if only I'd known this at the start'!

So she decided to do something about it and share the mumhood wisdom that only comes from experience with those who've got all that joy to come.

She is author of 'Learning Without School' and 'A Funny Kind Of Education' – another story of raising children but with a twist on the school years.

Find out more about her and her books here: http://rossmountney.wordpress.com

Copyright Ross Mountney 2013

All rights reserved. No part of this publication may be reproduced or transmitted in any form or by any means, including electronic or mechanical, information storage or retrieval systems, without prior permission from the author.

mumhood

how to handle it

why it matters

What you'll find in this book

Introduction

Chapter One: Becoming.....1

Becoming a mum is incredibly beautiful, important, challenging. This chapter is all about you being one, how to handle it right from the start and why it matters. There are Tip-Bits in between chapters to help you with your gorgeous child.

Tip-Bit No 1 - Crying Babies.....15

Tips on coping with a crying baby.

Chapter Two: Bodyshock.....19

The birth of a baby is a physical body blow. This chapter is to help you understand and suggests ways to nurture it back to what it was.

Tip-Bit No 2 –Sleep.....38

Suggestions on handling sleep – the child's and yours!

Chapter Three: The Emotion Ocean.....43

Did you ever feel so inexplicably emotional as when you become a mum? Here's a look at how mumhood can make you feel and ways to try and cope.

Tip-Bit No 3 – Breast, Bottles and Bananas.....64

Tips on feeding your child without fuss.

Chapter Four: Job Description.....69

Your workload seems to terrifically expand when you become a mum. This chapter shows how to recognise, prioritise and cope with the magnitude of work you do.

Tip-Bit No 4 - Nappies and Beyond.....86

Tips on nappies, loos and managing it all.

Chapter Five: Role-overview.....91

Your role as a mum may not be what you first thought of. Here are some ideas to help you think it through and choose how you want to play it.

Tip-Bit No 5 – Tantrums.....105

Understanding and coping with them.

Chapter Six: Great Expectations.....110

You have enormous pressure from hidden expectations when you're a mum. This part helps you wise up to them and choose ways to cope.

Tip-Bit No 6 - Ages and Stages?.....130

Managing expectations about your child's progress.

Chapter Seven: Mumworth.....134

Did you know how much you matter as a mum, not only to your child but to everyone? This chapter tells you how much.

Tip-Bit No 7 – Social Interaction and Other Illusions.....148

Understanding your child's interaction with others.

Chapter Eight: Mother and Child.....154

The best thing of all about being a mum is the relationships with your child. This chapter gives suggestions on making it one you'll enjoy forever and why that matters.

Tip-Bit No 8 - Naughtiness and Punishments; why kids do what they do and how to change it.....173

Tips for managing behaviour.

Chapter Nine: Ongrowing.....182

Your journey through mumhood is an ongoing one. This shows how to handle it as your child grows.

Tip-Bit No 9 - How You Influence Your Child's Education.....202

How to have a good effect on your child's learning from now and in the future.

Introduction

It's taken a while to do this book. And there's a good reason for that.

Firstly, the things I wanted to tell you about motherhood needed to mature a bit. When you first become a mum you can be raw, emotional and elated at the same time and I didn't think I'd be a lot of help like that!

Secondly, mumhood is no small simple matter; it takes a while to see it objectively enough to understand it. And I also now know that no one can tell another person how to be a mum just because they've done it; it's too involved and complex for that. As complex as our own individual personalities.

Each of us is different. Each of us has different characteristics, different skills and attributes, needs and wants, strengths and weaknesses. But, actually, that's okay. Our kids are all different too and need different kinds of mums and that's what this book celebrates.

So rather than mould us all into being the same this book acknowledges our differences and how we can each do our own special job of mothering in our own special way and still make it good. And it suggests ways of coping whilst you do.

It also celebrates the delectable joy we can have being mums. It celebrates how important we are, how much we matter, how amazing is the work we do and how simple it is to be good mums even with these complexities.

For being a good mum is not about getting it right all the time, it's not about doing it right or wrong or anything like that.

It's just about being yourself; growing the person 'you' who is also a mum, being loving and kind and responsible. And building a mumhood you can be truly proud of and deeply enjoy.

Chapter One

Becoming

It would be so easy, wouldn't it, if simply having a baby taught you all you needed to know to become a mum?

Having a baby does of course make you a mother in the physical sense of the word. But as most mums find out a little way down the mumhood road there's a lot more to handle than that. Adjusting to motherhood also takes a lot longer.

Just like baking a cake doesn't make me a cook, becoming a mum requires many more ingredients, experiences and skills than just giving birth. Not to mention practice. It doesn't just happen overnight and doesn't always happen naturally either. And becoming a mum who knows how to handle it and feels valued in doing so, is even more complicated.

That's why this book is here. This book is to help you understand these difficulties. It is to guide and support you in your mumhood because, just like your baby, you need time and encouragement too. This book is intended to nurture you while you do it for I suspect that you'll be so busy nurturing your baby you may well forget to do that for yourself.

Something very important

From the beginning, before all the more complicated bits, there's one aspect of being a mum that really matters. Yet the remarkable thing is, it's an aspect that most mums don't know about, they don't appreciate, nor even think about it much. It's rarely mentioned when anyone ever talks about motherhood. It's not rated, not respected in social circles - definitely not in male circles or politics, even though it is political really (not that I intend to bore you with politics here). Yet it is a simple and fundamental truth and basic ingredient for growth into a satisfying mumhood.

And that is: *understanding its enormous value.*

Looking back over our lives we usually recognise the things we do which are of value. It might be getting good grades. It might be helping a friend. It might be having a job or career. It might be love from, or loving, a boyfriend or partner, or our own parents. All these things we do we recognise as being of value.

Yet what most people fail to acknowledge, or even see, is the enormous *value of being a mum*.

Why does that matter?

Because mums are a group of *the most important people on the planet*. It is mostly mums - (and I say mostly because, although there are some absolutely great dads playing a vital role in the raising of their children, it is still mostly mums who do it) - who are responsible for seeing to the early growth and development of not only a child, but a new member of society, of the human race.

And why is that great?

Simply because this new person has the potential to contribute something. And they are part of a generation who will be responsible for the next generation, who will be responsible for the next, and so on. And, in the wider picture, these generations of children will grow into people who are responsible for the planet on which we live, thus being in charge of the perpetuation of all life. And this all starts with the nurturing of babies and children, most of which is done by the mums. This is what mums do. How great is that?

Your work with your baby and child is going to have an effect on everyone *ever after*.

So you can see how important your role as a mum is. (More on this later). You're a *parent* now and through the parenting of your baby or child you *will make a difference to the world*.

That is its value. That's why mumhood matters.

Understanding, recognising, and appreciating the *value* of your work as a mum has a huge effect on how you feel about it. This in turn affects what you do, how you do it, and your overall contentment as a mum.

When I say contentment it doesn't mean that there's something wrong with you if you're not content with being a mum - not everyone is. Or that everyone should be content with it all of the time, or that you have to be a mum to the exclusion of everything else. Mums may be mums, but they are other people too. Contented mums are contented *people* who do other things, have other work, are not necessarily with their children one hundred percent of the time (also important) to the exclusion of everyone else. They are not servants to their family, *nor are they any less of a person because they may not be earning.*

When I say contented mums I mean mums who feel able to *make choices* about what they do and feel good with their choices, who are confident with who they are now, what their work is about and why it matters, who are balanced rounded people in their mumhood and therefore able to make a good job of it, rather than someone smothered by the enormity of it.

For it is an enormous step becoming a mum, there's no doubt about that, and to become at ease with it takes time and involves lots of readjustments to life, lots of rethinking, lots of reprioritising and lots of mood swings.

This book is here to help you cope with all that. It gives you lots of things to think about. It discusses issues that many motherhood books overlook, tending to be all about the baby and forgetful of mum. Yet these issues hugely affect your satisfaction with mumhood. Things like:

- The shock of the birth
- Your emotions
- Your new workload
- Your new role as a mum
- The expectations you have to cope with
- Your enormous worth as a mum
- Your relationship with your child
- Your ongoing journey

These are some of the things you have to think about when you become a mum. These are some of the things you have to cope with which are often overlooked when we get advice on coping with nappies, or breast feeding, or bathing a baby, or dealing with tantrums.

Now I'm not underestimating the value of advice on dealing with these things. They all have to be coped with too and at the end of each chapter I include some tips. But there are already many excellent books giving information on babies and children.

This book is different. It is almost exclusively about YOU – the mum – and helping you handle the things you have to go through and which things matter.

Helping you cope

Becoming a mum is challenging. Lovely – but challenging. There's a lot to cope with. A lot to cope with *personally* – never mind coping with a baby.

We have to cope with the birth process, which is an enormously understated shock to our systems, one which we often don't get the opportunity to fully recover from as we launch into life with the new baby.

We have to cope with our emotions and spirits as they resettle themselves after a hormonal upheaval that's akin to a tsunami.

We have to cope with our relationship with a stranger - our new child!

We have to sort out what our role is now both in the home and out of it and the shared workload – if we're lucky enough to have someone to share it with.

We have to sort out what our job of being a mum entails, this job that we've never done before, there's no real training for and certainly no job description making it clear cut and simple. In fact it's a job that isn't written down anywhere, isn't established and is forever changing. It doesn't have boundaries, knock off time, lunch and coffee breaks and sometimes continues throughout the night. It's no small task.

We have to cope with our position in society, where judgements, expectations and criticisms seem to be freely given without us asking for them and everyone seems to be able to do it better, especially the relatives. We have to cope with how our identity changes.

Handling all of this is hard and can make us mums upset and is it any wonder? Especially when we are not even aware of the enormity of it. It's enough to make the toughest of us crumble.

Add onto that the fact that you as a mum today also have it a lot tougher than mums used to. Because there are a lot more decisions to be made than there used to be and a lot fewer hands around to hold the baby while you adjust.

There are lots of choices open to mums now which our own mums, and their mums before them, never had, consequently they never had to make the decisions associated with them. Modern developments in society and culture, which are such a blessing freeing women from many of the restraints that came with womanhood, can also be a burden of decision making and a bane to parenting and satisfying mumhood.

For example, the opportunity for women to have a career as well as children is a deserved right for today's women. But it can also tear them apart when decisions and choices have to be made. Another example; new developments in technology and connectivity are wonderful as is the opportunity of being able to find immediate answers online, but it can also be a mountainous dilemma of parenting when you have to regulate your child's use of it never mind the pull of social networking that draws time away from our mothering.

Choices in products and parenting approaches are mind-boggling, the multitude of them extended by the Internet so much we're almost overloaded with information and ideas. It takes hours surfing and connecting online, hours which might have been spent just holding and connecting with your child.

Freedoms and rights that our children now have are very welcome and right, but they also make parenting more demanding and challenging than it ever was now that those old fashioned unseen codes of conduct, behaviour and respect, that were inherent in community and helped guide our children, have been eradicated.

None of these decisions and challenges to motherhood our forbears had to deal with. And the decisions they did have to make were usually supported by a close network of wider family and community members all on hand which few of us have now. Forums, although comforting at times, just aren't the same.

These are the kinds of things that make it very tough to be a parent. Tough to cope with. Even tougher to be a mum who is clear about her role, confident in her choices, and happy with the work she does.

This book contains some ideas that will help you cope with all those things.

Not good advice

Now this may seem a bit odd but this book is not about giving advice.

This is because I'm not one of those mums who maintains she knows how to do it better than you – I freely admit that. I'm an ordinary mum. A mum who's been through it, a mum who's had a variety of experiences with children in different settings, a mum who's thought loads about it. But I'm definitely not dictating what you should do and there's a good reason for that; it's not helpful.

The ideas here are just ideas. Ones you need to chew over as you have coffee with another mum friend. They need chewing over. For you need to develop *your own ideas*. That's what will help you grow and help you do what's best for you and your child, rather than someone dictating to you.

The only advice that I'd like to suggest, over and above everything others tell you, is to listen to *your own gut feeling*.

No one knows the situation you're in better than you. No one understands your child better than you. You will begin to know how to work things out and your intuition will know what's best for you. You are unique, your situation is unique, trust your instincts. One of the best things about being a mum is that you can get almost primeval instincts to guide you. It's best not to ignore them – balance them by talking with others, but pay attention to what they're telling you. This takes practice – it will come with time, hopefully this will support you whilst that happens.

But to write a how-to-do-it handbook on being a mum would be an insult to all the idiosyncratic ways women out there mother their children. I don't want to interfere with that. Children need their own mums. Your child needs you to be the mum you need to be. To be the person you need to be – if you could now identify who that person is.

The person 'YOU'

This is another reason why this book is here. For there appears to be many mums who are not sure who they are when they become mums and not clear about what they should be doing.

Instead there are mums who are confused and find it hard to relax into mumhood. Who find it hard to enjoy themselves, fail to understand the *value* of their position and who miss the *joy* in the miracle of their children. There are many mums who just seem to be tired, run down, worn out workers in conflict with what their inner feelings and outside pressures are telling them. In conflict with being a mum and another person too. In conflict with what they feel they should be doing and what they feel others think they should be doing.

Becoming a mum isn't easy. It is sometimes not always what you choose to be. But if you're a mum you might as well enjoy it. What you need to do is unwrap that hidden agenda that comes packaged with motherhood, notice what's making you feel less than content with it, change the way you think about it, and maybe lead life a little differently.

Above all *value it* for the important job it is and the contribution you are making to society through doing it and what that means to you. This will start the process of you changing into a person who is now also a mother.

This is another important concept; the fact that you are still a *person* as well as a mum. Something you need to keep at the forefront of your thinking because it's often *the person you* that gets neglected in favour of always being the mother you.

A little story

I and all my mum friends said the same things over and over about becoming a mum:

a) we were confused about integrating who we used to be with who we were becoming, almost to the point of bereavement;

b) although we found books and advice helpful some of them made us feel totally inadequate when we could not achieve the high ideals of motherhood bliss so often portrayed;

c) we all felt that so much of what we now understand about motherhood – that is, about becoming a mother as much as doing a mother's job – was never discussed in any of these books even though it's of vital importance;

d) a few years down the line we now all say - despite being so immersed in it at the time - it all changes SO quickly, every crisis gets over, and it's SO important to be the person and mother you want to be.

The *person you* is making a journey. It's a journey that is often fraught, worrying, often filled with landmines and pitfalls, often rocky. But then, that's the same in all life, isn't it? And the thing is, it also has the potential for such *joy and love* underneath the worry.

Handling worry

There is never a time in a woman's life when the potential for love is so great. Unfortunately the love and joy sometimes gets buried under worry and we can't feel it. That's normal. We all do it.

A new job is a worry – this is a new job. Unsettled hormones don't help.

A good way to cope is to first *identify* exactly what the worry is by asking: a)is it a *realistic* worry; b)is it something that *really is* going to happen, or c) is it just something that your mind and imagination is blowing up *out of proportion* and will probably *never* happen anyway.

It's amazing how much worry we can conjure up through our imaginations about something which *might* happen, but which *isn't* happening, and has about as much chance of happening as me being asked to star in the next James Bond movie.

Here are some of the classic things all mums worry about but which *hardly ever* happen:

- Being an awful mother
- Being unable to cope
- Ruining your child
- Doing everything wrong
- Making dire decisions
- Being emotional, neurotic and sad
- Not knowing what to do

Now I know it's easy for me to say 'don't worry' because I've passed through many of the stages I worried about. But what I've learned as a result is that *none* of these worries above, which I wasted an awful lot of time worrying about, came true. It was me getting things out of perspective.

Thinking about worry:

Let me give you a logical take on why none of the above worries will come true.

You're a thinking mum or you wouldn't be reading this. A thinking mum is a mum who learns and therefore could not be an awful mother because in the end a thinking mum always copes somehow even if some of the time she doesn't. A mother who copes is not a mother who necessarily has to cope all of the time, but she never ruins a child for she thinks about her actions and she listens to others. She makes contact with others who help her keep things in balance and help when she feels neurotic and sad as all mums do some of the time. She deals with the responsibility as she gets used to it, gets to the right decision in the end even if she makes changes after making the wrong decision, something we all do.

This is how you will avoid all the classic worries above and how it will work out for you; just by being a thinking mum. Remember; *it is always okay to ask.*

And finally, worry is based on the future. Concentrate on this moment *now*, and let the future take care of itself.

Being a 'good' mum

Lots of women worry about being a 'good' mum. It's not surprising; there are plenty of ideals and images in the media about what a 'good' mum is.

There's a 'Supermum' image of a woman who can do everything; raise a child, have a stunning career, look fantastic all the time, keep an immaculate house and never wear a pair of joggers or have body fat. Definitely not me.

There's the 'perfect' mother image of baking, cleaning and contented domestic bliss, which can make those who find domesticity about as fulfilling as cutting your toenails feel totally inadequate.

Then there's the mother committed to one hundred percent attachment which makes me feel positively neglectful and guilty should I want to be away from my children sometimes or sleep with the children's father.

And there are all the celeb mums who look so stunning, make it sound so glamorous and easy, they frankly make me feel like a bag lady.

So many different and very influential images of what a 'good' mother should *look like*. But although there may be elements of all of them in our mothering, the problem is that being a 'good' mother has nothing to do with what you should look like, or when you decide to finish breast feeding, what nappies you use, or the image you portray. Because becoming a mum is not only about doing a good job, it entails *being good person*. It is all about how you should *be* and nothing to do with how you should appear. Being a good mother is about that; *being*.

But how should you be?

To be a good mum is really very, very simple. It has nothing to do with appearances. Nothing to do with good grades or qualifications. Nothing to do with anything you can buy, your wealth, your assets or your income. And even better it is something that is easily available for *all* women to be if they so choose.

Being a good mother is simply about being a *good, loving human being*.

That's all it takes. Just being a good human being who cares for herself, her child and other people, her own home and the wider world, who thinks about what she's doing and is prepared to keep an open mind, grow and learn new skills when necessary, communicate with others. That's all it takes to be a good mum. A good mum is just the extension of being a good, caring human being. That's all you need to be to get it right.

So rather than worry, the best thing to do is to grow some trust in YOU.

Good news

The good news is that behind all the worry there is always love. Love is part of the package of being a mum. As a mum you get loved loads – as long as you're not worrying and fussing too much so you miss it.

You get that gorgeous response as your baby begins to recognise you. You get that wonderful smile when they first can do it. You get outstretched arms when you get home and little limpets round your knees. Then your waist as they grow. Then your shoulders or cheeks to cheeks when they get to the height mine are now.

Delicious! Don't miss out on it because you're busy fretting about imaginary anxieties. Keep sight of the loving bits; they make up for the worry. Love and worry can be an equal burden sometimes. But the love your children give you is beautiful, unparalleled, worth working for. Motherhood, love, babies, children; they're all worth it. Revel in it, it changes fast.

I hope throughout this book to help you do that for sometimes it is difficult to see when motherhood gets tough. And it does get tough; it can get confusing and overwhelming. But there is *always* someone you can turn to, someone who's been through it before, someone who can help.

Sometimes mums can feel isolated. This is often not so much about the physical isolation of being at home with a baby when you may have been used to the interaction of work every day, but the way you feel about approaching another person for help. Mums sometimes feel ashamed about asking for help from others.

There is absolutely *no shame* attached to saying to another mum 'I'm struggling with this right now, what would you do?' so get networking. Start online with mums groups (e.g. Netmums and Mumsnet) and progress from there to meetings etc. Most mums you come across are very happy to help – after all, they know what it's like. And if you're interacting with mums who are not, then change them.

Being asked to help by another mum is an honour. It recognises and shows appreciation to another person – so give another mum that honour when you need help and ask them. And one day you'll be able to do the same for someone else. For in the wink of an eye you'll realise how fast your baby grows and you're the one with experience able to help others.

Becoming a mum is a monumental metamorphosis. Take time to grow into it. Take time to enjoy the loving bits. Take time to think about it. Give yourself time to adjust and rethink. Give yourself time to work out what it is that's going to make you the mum you want to be. This time of your life is as much about YOU as it is about babies and children. It is about becoming reasonably content with the wonderful mayhem of motherhood. You and your child will be developing together.

Tip-Bits

Having said all that, no one is going to be content when they've got a baby or child who isn't. So, at the end of each chapter I include a few tips about you and your child. They are in chronological order and grow with kiddie stages.

These are just thoughts and ideas that other mums and I found helpful. What's important to remember is that they are just tips. They are not gospel truths. Or advice set in stone. And they can be totally ignored if you wish for what works for one mum does not always work for another. That's just the way it is – it's not something you need to worry about.

That's the snag with advice; if it doesn't work it's easy to worry you're doing it wrong. Instead of realising the truth of the matter which is; *it's just different for you*.

You will begin to understand what's best for you and your baby most of the time. You will begin to listen to your intuition. If you're stuck for ideas, try the tips. But remember to keep them in the perspective of the intuitive feelings you already have. Compare them to what others say. Seek expert help if you're not sure. Gut feelings often work out to be true.

Finding your way with mumhood is a matter of trial and error. That's how everyone learns. There's no reason why you can't learn too. Just trust in yourself.

This is all going to take time and you may be feeling you need to do something right now to help yourself cope with being a mum. And there is something you can do right now. You can establish a habit of *looking after You*.

Looking after You

One of the most effective steps you can take towards becoming a fulfilled person and good mum is that simple one: look after yourself. You'd think this was so simple that it doesn't need working out at all. But it needs working at.

The reason I'm bringing this to your attention is because it is an aspect of their lives that many mums are bad at. They're fantastic at looking after their child. But in doing so they neglect to look after their own needs too. The 'looking after' priority becomes the child.

This really is as silly as running the central heating but never overhauling the boiler or topping up the gas or oil. We wouldn't do it. Yet I see many mums who are giving their child heaps of looking after but never give any to themselves. They prepare nourishing food for their child but just snatch a biscuit for themselves or a mug of caffeine. They carefully schedule in the baby's nap but never rest themselves. They provide stimulation for their child and take them out but fail to provide for their own needs in this department. And they often do all this out of obsession with creating an *image* of a good mum and what others will think, rather than what's really important for them or their child.

It's silly really but easily done – yes, I've done it too, until I realised. I clicked how important it is to look after myself *as well as the child*. Looking after your child will take up an awful lot of your time and energy. It's important to save a little for you.

It is also important because it is part of what I said earlier about value. Valuing the job you do is valuing you as a person doing it. A mum who values herself, *values herself enough* to make sure her needs are met. A mum who does not have her needs met will struggle to be a good mum. It is much harder to be a good mum if you are feeling neglected, run down, worn out and discontent; it soon breeds resentment when you feel like that. Resentment breeds impatience and anger, reflects on your parenting and sometimes even leads to abuse of children. It is essential not to get to that point because of self neglect. A habit of self care helps prevent this from happening. It will also help with baby blues if you attend to you as well as your child.

A habit of self care is also important for another reason. You want your child to be happy. A child who has a happy and fulfilled mum is usually a happy and contented child. A child who sees his mum looking after herself will learn to look after himself, and others too. He will learn how important self care is.

Self care is not about selfishness to the exclusion of others. Self care is sensible. It is simply about looking after yourself as you would look after others. Self care is the basis for self esteem and confidence as your child grows. Self care is part of the growing and learning process you demonstrate to your child and the foundation of caring for others. It is part of humanity, part of caring for one another, part of developing happy, contented people.

Happy, contented people are people who make up a good society. Happy, contented people are usually the ones who look after each other, are considerate towards others and responsible towards the planet. They are generally not the ones who commit crimes against each other, abuse or violate the planet.

This is why it's so important to raise contented, joyful children who feel good about themselves. And this nearly always starts right at home with mum, with a fulfilled mum. By adopting this habit of caring for yourself you will create a ripple effect throughout the whole world. Just think of that!

Here are some ideas to get you started:

- Pay as much attention to your own needs as you do your child's.
- Introduce small pockets of time when your child understands that they will not be getting your attention for half an hour and make sure they have an activity available which may well mean accepting help from others.
- Understand it is as important to accept babysitting help to enable you to get some rest as it is to accept babysitting help while you go to work or the supermarket. It is justified.
- When you lay your child down to rest, forget the jobs, lay yourself down to rest too.
- Rethink your priorities about other things that are perhaps less important right now like tidy house, immaculate surfaces, clean car, bursting social calendar. You and your baby need big chunks of your time for a while. Something has to give. That's okay - it will change.
- Feed yourself well with nourishing foods rather than junk foods. Accept help in preparing them.
- Give yourself some time for your own grooming and pampering, soak in a bath, hair do, massage, whatever you like.
- Dress how you like and in what you enjoy. Comfort and convenience may be your priority at the start and that is fine. It will change.
- Think about your part of the day as well as your child's. Make sure you schedule time for your own stimulation as well as everyone else's.
- Try and keep other things in your life besides mum things, even if it's just reading a book or magazine, fitness class, coffee with friends.
- Make a habit of thoughts for You. Being a good mum is about being good to yourself too.

Tip-Bit No. 1: Crying Babies.

One of the hardest things to deal with at the start of being a mum is an incessantly crying baby.

I was one of the lucky ones for although my babies cried - all of them do, it wasn't incessantly, they did stop. But it usually took a lot of walking about with them for ages – just what you need of an evening when you're dead tired. But it was not as bad as the ones I heard about who didn't seem to stop, whatever their parents did.

To have a baby like that is truly stressful. And if yours is doing that you have my sympathy. There are two things you need to keep in mind while you're going through it that will make it a bit easier for you to bear.

Firstly; this phase will end – all these baby phases do. (Not counting those infants who are truly ill and before you worry, there are relatively few of those).

And secondly; it's *not* because you're a bad mum.

Some babies cry incessantly because they are ill, and there are causes, and you may want them checked out by a doctor. But it is a well known fact that some babies just cry incessantly for no obvious reason. And there's nothing you seem to be able to do to stop it.

You will no doubt have read online about all the tried and tested ploys mums have used to ease their baby from crying. Things like holding them close, singing or talking to them, music or the television, the noise of the vacuum or washing machine. Taking the baby for a walk or putting them in view of things blowing in the garden. Company, other children, mobiles or other such distractions.

But sometimes, with some babies, these things do not work. So perhaps it might help to accept that your baby is one of these and think instead of ways to help yourself cope with it. Because coping with it is tough and you are justified in getting help to give you a break. You will need to take care of yourself to get through it. And not beat yourself up about it being because you are a bad mother.

I have heard that after a while these babies do stop, often without any reason, but that's little comfort while you're going through it. Until then, get as much help as you can to cope with it.

Some mums feel bad about asking for help. But an incessantly crying baby is one of the most stressful things you have to cope with in the early stages and it is almost impossible to stay sane in the same room all the time with a baby crying. You may feel it's a lot to ask of someone else. But remember that they will be able to hand the baby back so a short time looking after your baby will do them no harm and will give you a much needed break. It is better to ask for help than to get desperate which may put the baby in danger.

If help isn't on hand you can put the baby in a safe place for a short while, perhaps the cot, and close the door so you can't hear. Again, it's better to do this than to become desperate. It is not an ideal solution but it won't harm your baby to cry for a few minutes and it's worth considering that it may harm your baby if you do not get a break and become stressed, desperate, or ill yourself. Remember; happy mums usually make happy babies. Keep repeating; 'this phase will end'.

Not all babies cry incessantly, thank goodness. There is the other kind; those that cry as per norm – when they want something. It could be feed, comfort, company, stimulation, sleep. You'll soon learn to recognise what they want and what to do about the cries.

When your baby cries she's asking for something in the only way she knows how. Some people believe that we should not always pick up or respond to a baby crying. But I soon learned to understand what my baby wanted, even if it was just contact and reassurance, and I decided that was a reasonable request. After all, many adults go through all sorts of peculiar motions to get attention and reassurance. I don't see why my baby should have her requests denied. And despite me doing all the holding, carrying, cuddling and comforting I think all babies need (actually all humans need), my children didn't turn into the annoying, demanding attention seekers the Health Visitors seem to live in fear of. In fact, that same health visitor, when visiting my second child, remarked upon how good the first was; 'she isn't attention seeking at all, is she?' I didn't tell her that this was because I'd ignored her advice and tended to her when she cried. But I believe that it was exactly because she had her cries answered that she found no need to demand attention – a child is more demanding when ignored.

Babies need to cry to tell you something until they master the use of language to do it for them. The funny thing is that if you watch adults, they have all sorts of annoying attention seeking behaviour and they do have the use of language!

Crying is the only way babies have of expressing their need for something. The trick is to decipher what that something is:

Hunger. One of the most common causes, easily rectified, although if it's only ten minutes since the last feed you might want to consider your reaction. Feed when you feel right about doing it. Don't be a slave to advice – or a slave to your baby. It's up to you what decisions you make about that – there's more on feeding in another tip-bit.

Comfort. And why not? We all need comfort. The baby is only little. Sometimes it's the human need for closeness that's required. We're lucky, we can get up and go partake of physical contact with another human being. A baby can't, they cry instead for a hug. Who could fail to respond to that?

Boredom. I think it must be extremely boring lying on your back all day watching the same piece of ceiling whilst extremely interesting life, which you can tantalisingly hear but not see, passes you by.

Any baby with a brain is soon going to get fed up with this – I would too. So you need to do something to interest him, like using a sling to do things with you, carrying him in various positions, prop him somewhere safely where he can see your face, talking or singing to him even if it's only about washing up. It's all fascinating to a baby – they haven't come across it before.

I always responded to a bored cry. I can't stand being bored. I couldn't commit my baby to that. Babies do need stimulation and interest for some of the time.

Sleep. Some babies actually need to have a little cry and a grisly time to get themselves to sleep. I didn't realise this and was busy bouncing mine about when all she wanted was to be left to sleep and needed to whimper for a few minutes to do it. If you choose to try this you will need to make a decision about how much and how long you want to leave them crying. And there's a difference between crying themselves gently to sleep and all out bawling in distress which I wouldn't ignore. You'll get to work it out with experience. It's a lot easier to have babies used to getting themselves off to sleep on their own, but some parents prefer not to leave them crying and always remain with them. And another word about stimulation; although stimulation is important some experts are now saying that babies can also be over stimulated, making it difficult for them to settle to sleep. Which all goes to show that fads among the experts come and go and it really is a matter of trial and error getting it right for your baby. Don't be afraid of getting it wrong during this process – you'll get it right as a result.

Discomfort. Lots of things can make a baby uncomfortable; wet or dirty nappy, something chaffing, too hot or too cold, clothes rubbing, something sticking in. Or the baby needs a change of position. You'll long for them to be able to tell you and it will come.

Ill or in pain. There comes a time when none of your usual recipes to stop your baby crying will work and you suspect there's something else wrong. If you're really concerned ring someone up, friend, clinic, doctor, and trust your guts. There are signs when a baby is ill like hotness, cold extremities, thrashing legs, limpness, abnormal cry or whimper, unusual behaviour, unusual nappy contents. Never be afraid to get advice when you're unsure. There'll be times when you need it, as we all did.

For the most part you'll get to understand what your baby is crying for and how to answer those cries. You know him best, you live with him all the time. Put all advice in the perspective of that. Time with him soon teaches you what their little cries are about and I don't think we need to be afraid of responding to them for fear of 'spoiling' the baby. The only 'spoilt' babies are neglected ones. There is a difference between giving positive attention and spoiling with obsessive fussing. You'll find the balance because it will feel right.

Your baby is only a small helpless baby for *a very* short time. You're allowed to love him to bits. You can't get enough holding and cuddling and nestling that soft head against your cheek. It's a valuable time for both you and him. It's the groundwork for your caring relationship, for your contented relationship. This won't spoil him. He won't get the better of you like this. Most mums say that this sweet, tiny holding time goes far too quickly and it's best to make the most of it while it's here. I miss it now. I'm glad I got as much as I wanted of it at the time. It was absolutely well worth every second.

Chapter Two

Bodyshock

Let me tell you a funny story. It starts one November night many years ago in our little cottage bedroom.

The night was quiet. My partner Charles snored gently beside me in the dark. There was no sound coming from the bedroom of our three year old. It was only me awake.

I looked at the clock; 3.30am. The tummy ache was strong. Perhaps I should get up and shave my legs.

Now you may be thinking that this was an odd thing to be doing at this hour of the morning, but I wanted to be perfect for the birth. And I had an inkling that this baby, which wasn't due till next week at the earliest, might be coming sooner just like the last one did.

I got up and went downstairs. It had been cold and we'd lit the open fire last evening. I gave it a good raking through looking for warmth and clattering loudly with the poker. If I'm honest I was hoping it would wake Charles up; I was in need of some comforting, not usually like me.

My tummy ache was stronger. I lay back on the sofa pulling a rug round my night shirt, not having the inclination to go back up and get my dressing gown. I drew my legs up under it away from the icy draughts that scoured the floor, deciding they'd have to stay stubbly for the time being – I'd do it later.

I heard Charles on the stairs.

"What you doing?" he asked, shambling into the room sleepily not really with it.

"I could be having a baby." I was trying to be funny but it came out more as a groan than a joke. I was beginning to feel very strange, not very in charge somehow which again was not like me.

His response was to turn away, pull back the curtain and look out into the black night; only it wasn't all black.

"Still snowing heavily," he said looking back at me and scratching his head. He always does this when he's thinking. "I'd better go get dressed." He disappeared upstairs again and came back down with his work suit on.

"I somehow don't think you'll be going to work today," I laughed, then quickly switched to gritting my teeth as another gush of even stronger tummy ache surged through me like an express. Only, I had to face the fact it wasn't tummy ache any more, it had identified itself as contractions, almost continual contractions. Just like first time round I seemed to have skipped all the preliminaries where contractions build up slowly and you get a bit of breathing space in between. This felt like full-on raging stomach cramps with extra twisting.

Charles picked up the phone to ring my mum to come and babysit as we planned.

"Don't rush," I heard him say down the phone through my semi-spaced consciousness, "the snow's falling heavily and the lane looks frozen."

And as if those words were the cue, it started for real. The second he said 'don't rush' the urge to push charged through me like the Eurostar, making me writhe about and moan uncontrollably – very unlike me.

Charles ignored me, as per usual for a man in an emotional crisis, and phoned the hospital, then went outside to start the car. He likes being practical. Between moaning I noticed a lot more head scratching.

My mum only lived about a mile and a half down the lane but never did it seem so long for her to come as I lay there writhing on that sofa trying not to be loud. The ache had gone to an intensity that was making me feel murderous and the contractions like one huge elephant bearing down inside. I tried and tried not to push but this wave of something far stronger than me took over and I felt as helpless as if I'd been trying to hold back the sea.

Charles kept dodging in and out, checking the car was still running, checking to see if he could see headlights through the blizzard, checking to see how I was doing, sprinkling me with snowflakes off his shoulders and ducking out again the minute I looked like a woman having a baby. He tossed me placatory comments that didn't console and I would have tossed back a stream of offensive language if I hadn't stuffed a cushion over my face so that any screaming wouldn't wake our firstborn sleeping right above.

Then, in a flash of sanity and wisdom between urges, the like of which I'm not usually prone to – but then, this was an unusual night – I realised I had to do something. I had to get my act together, get ready to go. I managed to pull on a pair of joggers over my night shirt and a pair of Charles' socks which were the only ones to hand. You can tell I was getting desperate.

Another uncontrollable urge and I scrunched up on the settee again with my teeth in the cushion. After that passed I grabbed a cardigan before the next one hit me. Still no babysitter.

By now I was certain the baby was actually coming but didn't believe myself. For like every good girl who'd watched the video and listened to the midwives, instead of listening to what my body was telling me, I believed everyone else who'd told me these things take time and mums know nothing. I should have learned from my last effort that I do it differently and to *trust my intuition*. Easy to say in hindsight when you're not hormonally mental.

Finally, mum arrived and two speckled snow-people emerged through my drama talking about towels and hot water and I was thinking they'd been watching too many old films. It doesn't happen like that in real life – or does it?

I braced myself for action after the next wave of contraction then, soon as it was over, hobbled out to the car without shoes on and threw myself on the back seat in an undignified heap. But I didn't give a toss; so much for the niceties of shaving my legs. I must have looked a sight but my only concern just then was how fast we could cover the ten miles to the hospital in a snowstorm.

We got stuck in the snow before we even got up the slight incline out of the drive.

Charles told me afterwards that that's when he started to panic too. I considered during my next sane moment getting out to push the car. After all, we could hardly ask the baby sitter, she was over seventy at the time. But another kind of pushing absorbed my attention and in the midst of full blown screaming Charles finally got the car moving and swerved out onto the road in a flurry of snow and another flurry of obscenities from me.

I'm afraid I behaved very badly then. I'm quite ashamed of it now. I don't usually behave like that – but I did tell you, it was rather an unusual night.

At that time in our relationship Charles wasn't even aware that I knew such language let alone said it out loud. And I can't begin to imagine how stressful it must have been for him driving that car and listening to me first screaming then hurling abuse from the back.

"Do you want me to stop?" he asked without daring to take his eyes off the road behind the snow clad screen.

"Course I don't want you to ******* stop, just get me to the ******* hospital. (Groan). Can't you go any ******* faster. (Scream)."

He didn't go any faster, brave man, because it must have taken some courage not to, but he'd already passed two cars in the ditch from the night before.

Ten minutes into the journey and I knew I was losing the battle with not pushing. The waters broke and as I rolled about on the seat trying to keep my weight off my pelvis there was an almighty force of pushing which I had no control over, and I knew the baby's head was born.

Dead silence. Stillness.

And an insight of desperate clarity when the pain all stopped and my sanity returned. My thought then was that this baby was not going to make it. Or worse still, was already dead.

I was unaware of any pain then. In a split second I just knew that I had to do something; this baby needed to be born.

Another monumental struggle to get an unshaved leg back out of those blasted joggers in case the baby suffocated. I braced myself with one leg shoved against the back door and the other jammed in the back window somewhere. And as another contraction seared through me, the car swerved violently round a bend sliding across the road and I pushed like hell. How I didn't push the car door out I don't know but the baby shot out onto the seat with the most almighty and reassuring wail.

The sound of that created absolute sobbing relief all round. But I knew we weren't out of danger yet.

I groped down in the darkness to get a hold of the slimy little newborn. It's amazingly difficult to tell which way is up when the pointy bum and head feel slitheringly similar. I drew the baby, (boy or girl?) up onto me, snuggling it against my body inside my cardigan, still wailing heartily, until we arrived triumphant at the hospital.

Charles went nonchalantly over to the hospital door and rang the bell. It took ages to get anyone to answer.

"The baby's already arrived", he said and suddenly their interest went up a few gears. A whole team of midwives were running out to the car. One climbed in with me, dealt with the cord, allowed me a kiss goodbye and the baby was whisked off to intensive care.

All that was left for me to do was to climb out, one bristly leg in one leg out of those wretched jogging bottoms, my night shirt soaked, only Charles' socks on my feet in the snow as I transferred to the wheelchair. So much for perfect for the birth.

And the irony of it is that Charles, whilst busy driving, missed actually 'seeing' the birth for the second time, since the first time he was busy throwing up out of the hospital window.

To put your mind at rest; **this is highly unlikely to happen to you.** My children's births are always fast and I'm just difficult, everyone always says so.

Baby Charley Joan, a little girl, soon recovered from the night with only hypothermia and continues to lead life in the way that she was born; at a determined rush.

Our first born has no recollection of the screaming only finding Granma in our bed in the morning.

Charles recovered from his dreadful night quickly enough to be able to clean the car ready for me to come home the following day, the gallant man.

For me, it took just a bit longer!

The shock of giving birth

This was a dramatic and traumatic birth. But actually, *so is every single one*. Your child's birth will have been. My first child's was. All births are. They are a *huge* physical and emotional upheaval.

That's not to say that they are not bearable, or not beautiful, or unbelievably magical too. But they are a physical blow to the body and an emotional shock to the spirits, the like of which we won't have experienced before no matter what kind of experience we have. Pain or not, perfect or not, they are all a shock. And recognising that is the first step to getting over it.

I had an accident once. To cut a long story short I got run over by a horse and cart. (Told you I was difficult).

But like with any accident that people suffer I was given lots of kindness, TLC, and sympathy not only for my injuries which were miraculously light, but also for the *shock*. In fact, people were more concerned about me recovering from the shock than anything else. They recognised that it was something I may need help with and I got lots of support to do so.

Having a baby can be an equally big shock, most particularly if it is a first baby. In fact, it is not just one shock, it is a series of after-shocks as other life-changing realisations reveal themselves. It's important you understand that in order to begin healing from this wondrous miracle of becoming a mum.

The wondrous miracle

If you think about it, right from the moment of conception growing a baby and giving birth to it is an absolute miracle. Our bodies are incredible to do it.

It's a natural miracle that's been happening since the beginning of man. It's as natural a part of a woman's life cycle as puberty, menstruating, menopause, as natural a miracle of evolution as any other biological miracle of any living organism. It is science at its best, biology at its best; something that mostly can occur without our interference or our intellect. It's awesome, as awesome as the inevitability of the seasons, or the fact that the earth keeps turning. That's the natural magnitude of it. Wow!

BUT, the fact is; *natural doesn't make it easier to handle. Or get over.*

Just because it's natural it doesn't make it any less traumatic or overwhelming. Maybe that is exactly why it's a shock, because it's often our first experience of the natural but overwhelming and physical *power* of our bodies to take away our normal control when the force of nature is at work. It certainly surprised me.

Simply because women's bodies have been experiencing this incredible upheaval - for that's what it is physically, natural or not - doesn't mean that's it's something we should just accept and get over as if it didn't have an impact. But sometimes, that's the way birth is treated. And sometimes, that's what mums expect of themselves. That they should just give birth, have a baby in their life, and carry on where they left off. And I would hazard a guess that you may have expected it to be like that. And one of the after-shocks mums experience is that you realise you were completely wrong.

Despite the fact that it's been going on for millions of years, each one of us will have had a unique birth experience. Some will have been natural, some will not and others will have had an enormous amount of intervention, but all give us a bit of a jolt, all come with the need to heal and adapt to being changed, as all experiences do change us.

To set ourselves up to handle everything mumhood throws at us from now on in depends very much upon giving ourselves some time to heal right from the start. To giving ourselves a recovery period, first physically, then emotionally, mentally, spiritually.

During this recovery period there are several things we need to do – not to mention adjust to life with this baby in it:

- We need to understand and appreciate what we've been through
- We need to look after ourselves
- We need to accept help and support
- We need to take our time
- We need to progress gently

Take a look at all you've handled so far

So many of the challenges we handle in order to grow and give birth to our baby get completely taken for granted. You can't appreciate what you need to recover from if you don't notice it in the first place. This list might give you some idea:

First, there's a lot of personal indignity which, to make it worse, often remains unspoken-

- Least of all mine; one leg in one leg out. Other women endure worse scenarios.
- The intrusion of having our body taken over for use by someone else (the baby).
- The intrusion of unpleasant examinations, sometimes at the hands of those who are less considerate or respectful than we would like.
- The indignity of losing control as powerful natural forces take over.
- The loss of our personal privacy, sometimes our personal rights, as others tell us they know better about our own bodies and what we're feeling than we do ourselves.
- The indignity of crying in public which we can sometimes no longer help and having to constantly ask where the ladies is!

Secondly, there are physical changes –

- Changed body shape and image.
- Changed skin and hair.
- Aches and pains, discomfort, strain on our organs, not to mention our tummy.
- The physical adaption as our bodies return to normal.
- Coping with bleeding and stitches.
- Changes in our weight.
- Coping with enlarged breasts and feeding.

Thirdly, the tiredness –

- Overwhelming, sometimes debilitating weariness.
- The start of disturbed nights.
- Sleep deprivation.
- The start of twenty four hour duties.
- The demands new motherhood puts upon us that are more tiring than any job we've done before.

Finally, the actual birth –

- The devastating physical upheaval.
- The endurance and stamina required.

- Injury from the birth like rupture, back strain, haemorrhoids, surgery, etc.
- The emotional upheaval which is probably greater.
- The fear, pain, stress and shock particularly if it didn't go according to plan.

Just think if someone handed you this list as something you would have to endure when you were applying for a new job anyone in their right mind would say 'get lost' and go for a different job.

I'm not suggesting we shouldn't do this job and this list is not here to discourage or terrify. It's here to illustrate how amazing we are in accomplishing what we do. It's here so that you really understand the enormity of what you go through to become a mum, because it is truly amazing. Only by acknowledging this, will you be able to give yourself some credit and see the need for a time of recovery.

Help yourself recover

Recovery doesn't only involve lying down to take the weight off your stitches, catnapping to make up for missed sleep or trying to get those extra pounds off. Recovery means looking after your state of mind and your spirits too.

To look after your mind and spirits you need to be mentally nice to yourself as well as physically. This means not expecting to bounce back and get on with motherhood as if nothing had happened. Not beating yourself up because you're taking longer than your friend did. Not worrying over the fact you feel so tired and feeble you can't even get dressed. Never telling yourself you're pathetic or similar.

I don't like to equate giving birth to an accident because it's nothing like it. But that's the only way I can think of to describe it so you'll understand how to look after yourself in order to recover quickly. If you'd had an accident you wouldn't expect to bounce back as if nothing had happened, you'd probably take it very easy, you'd be careful with your injured parts, you'd accept help and support from others, you'd relax, and you'd pamper yourself with little treats until you felt better. This is similar to what you need to do now.

The BIG snag is, of course, that after giving birth this is very, very difficult because there's someone else who is taking all your attention and who needs nurturing too; this new little dependant in your life.

And this is a critical point where many mums take the wrong turning and their mumhood is affected by it forever after, often making it an unending struggle rather than a pleasure. They make the mistake – actually two mistakes - of; a) lavishing all their care and attention on the baby and giving none to themselves, and b) never allowing themselves a proper recovery time. And actually, I've just thought of a third, c) not accepting any help that is offered in order for them to do so.

Some mums rush forward into coping mode, wanting to cope with it all themselves, wanting to prove what 'good' mums they are by seeming to do it all, wanting to manage without help because they think this proves something, or becoming so attentive to their new baby they never give a thought to themselves. And that's often very easy to do if you're as gobsmacked by the little being and in love with it as I was.

The trouble with all this is that it may appear to be fine at the outset. But the effects do not make themselves apparent until later on.

The effects of no recovery period, no attention paid to resting and getting over the shock of the birth, and one hundred percent attention to the baby and no attention to yourself, can sometimes manifest themselves into things like excessive tiredness, body not healing and returning to normal properly, depression, low self-worth, inability to cope, anxiety, unable to think and reason, getting things out of proportion, resentment, and even illnesses.

Now, we all suffer from those some of the time anyway. But they are exacerbated by not looking after your recovery whilst you adapt to your motherhood. By not appreciating what you've been through. And by not understanding that *your needs have to be looked after as well as the baby's*.

Just accepting a little offer of help is a great way of attending to your needs. And just remember the fact that the baby benefits more than anything else from a mother who is well and happy and who respects herself as a mum.

Respecting yourself as a woman who has just grown a baby, given birth and who is now a mother will promote an example of respect for all mothers. Building respect for women who have become mums will create a better life for mothers everywhere. What could be a better thing to be doing than that?

Coping with tiredness

Performing miracles takes some doing. It's no small task. And as a consequence leaves us with another shock to cope with – tiredness.

The overwhelming tiredness I experienced after becoming a mum hit me like another body blow. It was so unexpected particularly as I hadn't really felt it during pregnancy, or experienced it deeply at any other time in my life however hard I worked and played.

Physical tiredness, limb-heavy, deep down tiredness that is as cloying as any we may have experienced at work previously can be the most debilitating of all the physical changes we endure as we become mums.

We all know that physical tiredness is not conducive to contentment or happiness. It's difficult to feel good about something when you're tired all the time and when the very role you want to feel good about seems to be sapping all your energy. Feeling good needs energy. But being a new mum can sometimes sap all your energy and it can become a vicious circle that can spiral down into depression.

But it will change and you can help change it. This initial tiredness can be overcome if you pay a little attention to helping yourself over it. New motherhood is a series of phases. These phases change so quickly, which is comforting in a way, but overwhelming in others while you are trying to adjust to all the new demands thrown at you, for you will have the night feeding routines to cope with, anxieties about your baby, then a different demand as your child grows. Acknowledge and accept that these take some adjusting to. Work out ways to help yourself.

While you are going through these adjustments it might help to think about the following things:

Thinking about tiredness:

- Accept that you are tired. It is normal to feel tired, every other mum feels tired even the ones who don't admit it, there's nothing wrong with you feeling tired, it's not just you and you're not feeble. Give yourself understanding. Fighting it will not help. Accepting it and managing it will.
- Sleep deprivation is very hard – it's been used as torture that's how unbearable it is. During those first few weeks you will be suffering from sleep deprivation which has a huge impact on your ability to cope. Don't expect too much of yourself under

these circumstances. Take opportunities to catch up whenever they arise. It will soon alter.
- Remember all the miracles you have worked; the growth of your baby for nine months; the birth of your baby; the shock and physical demand of it; the mental and spiritual demand. When you look back at the list of things you went through it is no wonder you're tired. All miracles take their toll.
- Adjusting to new routines tire us all whatever they are. I don't know about you but whenever I started a new job I always felt very tired, not only with the new routine but more so with the new conscientious input I initially gave to it. It is exactly the same with becoming a mum, it's a new job and a new schedule and a huge new learning curve. Unfortunately it is also a twenty four hour job to get used to. No wonder you feel tired. It will become easier.
- Remember that you do not have to be Supermum. Your baby doesn't need an exhausted super hero. She needs a warm, loving, content and happy person. Listen to your needs, rest when you can, accept help when it's offered, to help you achieve this for both your sakes.
- Look after yourself.

The mistake some mums make is to think that they should be able to do it all themselves.

They think they have to do it all themselves because they're worried perhaps their own mothers will think they can't cope. They think they have to do it all themselves because their friends appeared to. They think they have to do it all themselves for fear of being seen to not cope. They think they have to do it all themselves because they held down a demanding job before and they can certainly hold down what it takes to be a mum. They think they have to impress the child's daddy. Etc, etc.

So many women think they are less of a woman, and less of a mum, unless they can do it all themselves. And this approach has created the myth of Supermum.

Who the hell's Supermum?

The myth of Supermum, who has a clean contented baby, who has a clean, ordered house, who has clean and stunning outfits, and who manages everything perfectly and still cooks delicious meals, has a fulfilling sex life and a perfect relationship and exercises regularly to get her body shape back whilst remaining sane, happy, and in control and doesn't even need help, is just that; *a myth*.

She doesn't really exist.

It is a myth because being this kind of super is just impossible. It's probably not even healthy. It's impossible to maintain and usually, when you come across people whose life appears to be like that, that's all it is; *appearances*. You don't get to see what's going on under the surface. Perfection doesn't usually go with real life, with real contented life either.

It's also a myth that wants exposing because it does mums an injustice. This is because it overlooks the fact that *all* mums who are doing the best they can are already *super*. However clean, or not, their house is. Whether they have a bursting social calendar or not. Whatever they choose to wear. Whether they cook or not.

Any mum who is adjusting to their new life as a mother, who is a good, caring person, who is managing to look after their new baby and who is doing that in the best way they can, is super. If we need the image at all.

Personally, I'd much rather be happy than be super. Happy, content mums raise happy content people who create a happy and content society. That's a great thing to be doing.

Just because there is dirt in the corners, decent meals seem impossible to prepare and we're living in our pyjamas for a while does not mean that we don't have standards. It just means we've had to change our priorities for a while. It means that we decide that our priorities might be different – i.e. attending to our child - accepting that this changes as our motherhood stages change.

Coping with tiredness, with looking after our new baby or child, looking after ourselves, need to be our priorities when we first become mums and go through these adjustments in life. Other things can take second place for a while – and it will only be a little while really in the course of a life - and we can return to them later.

Getting over our tiredness is important because it will set us up to cope better with what's ahead and therefore it actually makes us better mums. Wearing ourselves out trying to maintain model houses, immaculate outfits, perfect body shape and be a perfect manager of absolutely everything is unnecessary. These things are not as important to our baby, or to raising a child, as a good loving mum who is happy and not stressed.

These roles are discussed in detail later. Meanwhile since I brought it up perhaps it is a good moment to discuss the subject of body image.

Body image

Some mums find it hard to be happy when they are not happy with their body image. Giving birth can certainly play havoc with your body and that is something that needs coming to terms with.

Just like the image of 'Supermum' the image of the ideal body is also a *myth*. Because the image of the 'ideal' body only refers to *one* type of body – a skinny one with a flat stomach.

Just as there are all kinds of women and all kinds of mums there are all kinds of bodies. To try and make us all fit into one image totally disregards our diversity (and diversity is essential to the longevity of the human race – so we need diversity) and disrespects the millions of amazing women who do not fit into that one tiny category.

It is so important to remember and respect the facts that *all* bodies are shaped differently. *All* women carry their babies differently. *All* women's bodies adjust to childbirth in different ways. *All* mums are individuals. We would all be so much happier if we worked to that premise and not one created by the media that we should all be the same. Women are not skinny clones of one another; we are individuals and as individuals need to work to our individual body shapes whatever they are.

When you think about your body it is important to think of the *whole you*, your whole body, not just its shape in isolation.

The whole You

The *whole you* is made up of much more than just an exterior shape or your weight. It's a result of your genetic background. It is made up of all your organs and your bones. Your mind and your soul are part of the whole you. It is influenced by your diet and your life style. And it's important to think also of what *makes you happy* and keep that in the frame at all times.

So, when you think of your body shape think what's right for you in the context of all that. And try not to think of your shape, or weight, in isolation or in relation to what's portrayed in the media.

When you think of your body, rather than thinking only of your shape or what the scales say, think what's right for your *health;* physical, mental and spiritual. Your health is far more important than your shape and if you concentrate on your health, then the shape will find itself naturally.

For example, part of looking after yourself which I talked about earlier is looking after your health too. Your health is influenced enormously by what you eat. Eating too many fatty sugary junk foods is not a way of looking after yourself well. We all eat them occasionally because we mostly enjoy them. But we also need to balance that with eating good nourishing foods like fruit and vegetables, proteins and fibre in order to look after ourselves well. In order to respect these wonderful bodies and what they've just been through to give birth we need to nourish and rebuild them with foods that heal and build strength and energy not foods that harm or give us a quick fix then leave us feeling low.

Gradually reducing any excess body fat we don't want over a steady period of time is also another way of respecting our bodies and looking after ourselves well. Managing a healthy body weight is a part of looking after our health. Gentle regular exercise, when we are healed enough to do so, improves our physical and mental health. Exercising our bodies helps us cope better, it raises the spirits, keeps us fit enough to do the mum things we need to do, gives our kids the right messages. It doesn't have to be intensive labour at a gym. A walk a day with the baby or a few stretches at home are just as beneficial. But exercise is something that gives us confidence and helps us to maintain a healthy body. A healthy body is what we're after not a perfect shape. There's no such thing as a perfect shape or weight – we're all different.

If you respect your body as something that's tied up with the whole of your health then you will find the shape that suits you as an individual and it may not be the ideal portrayed in the media, but it may be a lot more ideal for you and it may make you a lot happier than some skinny image of perfection. Aim for optimum health; mental, spiritual, as well as physical, rather than an unrealistic body image. Aim for wellbeing rather than perfection. I recommend getting rid of the scales. You know how your clothes fit!

Not only will this help you, but it will also help to eradicate the unhealthy pressure put upon all women to uphold the media's image of perfect body image.

It would be so much better for mums everywhere, for children everywhere, those up and coming young girls included who are feeling the pressure to conform to this perfection and shockingly undergoing cosmetic surgery as young as nine, if we upheld health and happiness as our priorities over and above body shape.

Growing and giving birth to a baby changes our body shapes. But it is a skill our bodies undertake which we can be truly proud of. It's an awesome job we do. It's an awesome task we undertake when we become mums. It's much more awesome than being skinny.

Here are some things to remember when thinking about your body:

Thinking about your body:

- *You* are the important one not other people's image. That is – the whole you. Your health and wellbeing, your emotions and your spirits. Not just your body shape.
- If you look after yourself, as you look after your baby, if you give yourself time to heal, time for a little exercise and activity other than only being with the baby, if you feed yourself nourishing and wholesome foods as you would your family, your body will take care of itself. Concentrate on all your needs rather than just your body shape.
- Your body has performed a miracle. It has been worked hard and goes on being so as you feed, cuddle, realign your organs, do without sleep, heal any wounds. It is something truly to be proud of whatever shape it is.
- Give yourself some time. Give your body a break. It has just grown and given birth to a child. Enjoy and respect it for that. It's really something. Appreciate that some women are not lucky enough to have got that far.
- You're a mum. Not just a body shape. Mums are more important than shapes.
- Look after your body as part of looking after yourself. Look after what your body needs to keep it fit and well.

Whilst your body is healing

While your body is healing in that wondrous way it does, shifting its parts back into the right places, mending wounds, shrinking bits that have been stretched, gradually getting back to what it was before, you will be undergoing the next big shock on your journey to becoming a mum.

That is; your new life with your child.

It's a rather devastating, slow-to-materialise shock that takes a while to sink in. Sometimes you're so busy telling everyone about the birth and drooling over the new baby, and playing with all the new baby stuff you've bought that you fail to notice one very important thing; *this new baby is for life*. And life as you knew it before has just had one enormous dramatic change the like of which you had no idea about before.

<u>A little story</u>

My mum friends and I all felt that the sudden realisation that this whole new life as a mum was going to be completely different from anything we'd experienced before and from anything we'd anticipated was a far greater shock than the shock of the actual birth.

Giving birth changes you, but it is just not something you can anticipate, believe, plan, or be told about even though you've seen others go through it.

We've decided there's nothing you can do except be prepared to be unprepared; then adapt when you get there!

All the time you are pregnant, most of the classes you attend, most of the literature you read, tend only to concentrate on one thing; the birth and how to do it. Very little speaks of *life as a mum and how to handle it*.

This new life as a mum is probably very alien to life as you knew it before. You've changed; the birth will have changed you as every experience always does, not just physically either. Life has changed. And these realisations can be quite bewildering, often coming to you during the few days, weeks and months following the birth.

It can be quite hard to come to terms with this particularly if you were one of those people who were determined your life wouldn't change, the only change being that there was a baby in it. You'll soon realise it is not as simple as that.

This can leave you with the feeling of being completely overwhelmed, all consumed in a way you would never have imagined, sometimes even feeling cheated. Particularly if becoming a mum wasn't something you'd planned or were that happy about in the first place.

The turmoil of feelings which mums encounter is sometimes quite hard to deal with. There are new feelings, confused feelings, devastating feelings and all consuming feelings. And what's worse is these feelings seem to over take your whole life and you wonder if this is the only thing motherhood is about.

It isn't. And all these feelings do change.

Some of these feelings are down to tiredness. Some are down to hormones. Some are the result of circumstances. But *all* mums tend to experience them so it's comforting to know you're not the only one.

But what many mums fail to do is to address them.

Feelings are important. They tell us something. But they need sorting out so we can understand what it is that they're telling us and what we may need to do as a result. And that can make all the difference to being a good mum, a satisfied mum who enjoys the value of what she does.

The next chapter begins to discuss it. But before going onto that, if you're feeling overwhelmed at the moment, there are a few things you can think about to try and help.

Some tips to help with overwhelm at the start of your mumhood

- Relax. Rest as much as you can in the first few days.
- Rest properly, as in resting your mind as well as your body, look at a magazine, feet up or in bed occasionally.
- Going out on your own can be as good as a rest.
- Hand the baby over when you get the chance. Hand your child over. This is not shirking your duty as a mum. This is not not-coping. This should not make you feel guilty. You need to hand the baby over sometimes in order to look after yourself and be a good mum. One hundred percent contact is not necessarily good. An overwhelmed mum will find it hard to be a good mum.
- Give yourself the same TLC as you would your child. This way you value your rights the same as your child's rights and this

will be a good demonstration to them and the way they fit into the world. You teach them self-respect too.
- Share your birth stories with other mums. Talk to other mums – you'll find you're not alone.
- Remember you've performed miracles some women never have the chance to do. Miracles can take their toll.
- Allow yourself tears – there's no need to be ashamed. Shock makes you cry. Emotional upheavals make you cry. It's okay to cry, all mums do sometimes. I did. If you feel you can't stop, you're not the only one; don't be too ashamed to ask someone for help.
- Don't be afraid to speak to people about your concerns over your body healing, the changes you go through, how you're feeling. Remember these things change – it won't be like this for life. You're just adjusting.
- Don't set yourself unrealistic expectations. Accept how things are. Choose what you want to prioritise. These change as you grow into motherhood. Expect them to change. Reprioritise. Keeping flexible is what works best.
- Listen to your body. Do what is right for you. Be intuitive rather than manipulated by media images. But above all give yourself the respect of looking after your body properly. Remember that regular exercise is a great boost for both physical *and* emotional wellbeing.
- Healing takes some time. There may be a period of time – and this may come at any time during your motherhood not necessarily immediately after the birth – when you may feel overcome, you may feel cheated or frustrated, or angry at what's happened to you. This is quite normal. Talk about it. Accept it will pass. Work towards changing the way you feel to something more positive.
- Try and keep in mind an intention or visualisation of yourself having a fulfilled time with your motherhood and with your child. How *you* want it to be – not necessarily what everyone else is telling you it should be. This job you do with your child will be the most important thing you'll ever do (more on this to come). You'll need to feel it fits.

Babies are lovely, but they don't last. This is both a blessing and a shame. Enjoy your baby whilst it's small, it will never be like this again. Any difficulties always pass. Bodies always heal. Babies soon disappear into growing children. Life always changes so fast when you have children.

Tip-Bit No 2: Sleep

One of the biggest concerns that can consume a mum's every waking moment is the sleep concern.

This concern usually manifests itself into three big questions; how do I get my baby to sleep? How do I get him to stay asleep? And where should he sleep? And these are questions that apply right through childhood as the baby grows.

The shortest answer to this question, and one that's usually the result of our own desperation to get some sleep ourselves, is do whatever gives you an easy life! Remembering that whatever you do is going to change in a matter of weeks anyway as the baby grows and you're going to have to think of another plan.

During the first few weeks with the baby your whole existence can be geared to sleep, yours as well as the baby's. For if you can get the baby to sleep then you can get some. Never be afraid to nap in the day whilst the baby sleeps to catch up on yours, or enlist help so you can. You won't be able to function properly without it, so make sure you devote some time to your sleep too...but this section was about the baby.

All babies are different. Some babies just don't seem to want to sleep at all. Others are the complete opposite and sleep through the night very early on with a two hour nap in the day which is absolute bliss. Then there's a huge number of them who fall somewhere in between. So don't worry what your baby is doing, it's not a competition and there's nothing wrong if he is sleeping differently to your friend's baby.

But it's comforting to remember that if you have a baby who doesn't seem to want to sleep much at all, especially through the night, no matter how terrible the sleep deprivation you're suffering at the moment *things will and always change.* And they do so surprisingly quickly. All mums say that the baby phase goes so quickly; they're tiny for such a short time.

Meanwhile there are some things that mums have found worth thinking about when trying to get baby to sleep, assuming he's got a clean dry bottom and is otherwise comfortable. And these ideas lead onto happy sleeping patterns later on too when the baby becomes older.

It's worth thinking about *routines*. And it's worth thinking about *places*.

By routine I mean giving the baby set cues that routinely happen every night which help them to understand that it is time to lead up to something beautiful we all crave at the end of the day; going to bed.

It doesn't always work and it takes some time to establish but if you are consistent it helps in most cases. The earlier a pattern of behaviour you adopt for going to bed as an integral part of the day's routine the more used the baby will become to accepting that this is what they do next and it happens every day like that and they begin to fall into it easily. And you also need to demonstrate that after eight of an evening, for example, mum just switches off and there's not a lot of attention to be had.

You could establish a pattern like; tidy up of day's activities, gentle relaxing bath, little feed and cuddle, bit of telly (nothing violent or shouty – it's not time for you to watch Soaps) and story, then the baby is laid down to sleep. And mum becomes terribly inattentive, boring and ignores everyone and is quiet and calm. (Might take some doing, I admit!)

Going through this kind of routine every night soon establishes a set pattern which the baby will recognise and it becomes comfortingly familiar, also helping to calm them and help them drift off to sleep. Don't assume that just because they're a small being who can't talk yet they don't notice things like routine and what's going on around them – they do.

Your routine behaviour is as important as the routine for the baby. Your calm dwindling attention will help the child to understand that they are not going to get any more attention from you today, whatever horrendous behaviour they adopt, because it is sleep time. You need to adopt a kind of attitude that suggests that nothing else exciting is going on, it's time for sleep, you will be sleeping too.

It can sometimes be quite hard to do. Even harder to stick at. Because babies and children are really good at displaying reasons why they shouldn't go to sleep, getting kind caring mothers into a frenzy of worry about them, until you become absolutely convinced the baby is going to die the minute you leave them. Which hardly ever happens.

What usually happens is that babies begin to discover all sorts of different ploys that will keep you attentive to them a little longer. They are really quite reluctant to give up that attention they've been having all day – who can blame them? And sometimes mums find it equally hard to give up too!

Be reassured; babies are perfectly able to sleep on their own without you. Whether you want them to is another matter. Which brings me to the subject of where should they sleep?

Where you want the baby to sleep is a matter of personal choice. Some mums like a separate room for the baby. Some mums have a separate cot but in their room. Some like the baby in bed with them. And some families sleep all together for as long as the children want to.

It is up to you. Some things some mums find hard to do like having the baby separate from them others find easy, and some can't sleep with the baby in bed with them. There are advantages and disadvantages with all arrangements. For example, having the baby in the same room makes night time feeds easy. But not everyone can sleep. Some feel that having the baby in bed with you makes it hard if you want to move them out. Others don't find this a problem. Some feel that to make a baby sleep alone when we might prefer to sleep in company is cruel. Others say it's dangerous to have the baby in bed with you, particularly with a partner.

Whatever arrangements you decide on you must feel confident that it is right for you, your partner, the baby must be safe and comfortable, you must be safe and comfortable. After that, it really is a matter of personal preference and doing whatever makes it easier for you and makes the baby sleep well. But just think for a moment that routines established early are easier to keep. And preferences can change and circumstances can change.

Throughout it helps to establish routines and patterns the baby finds comforting. It's also helpful to be prepared to be flexible and change things if they don't work for you. Sometimes making these changes takes effort, but they are worth it to find a way of sleeping so that everyone gets the rest they need.

If you've got a baby or child who won't relax and go to sleep at the time you set for them it might be helpful to look at your routine, or how you are at bedtime, to see if there is anything you can change to improve things.

For example, walking about endlessly with a crying baby of an evening when you are very tired is enough to make anyone really wound up.

This atmosphere will be one the baby can sense and will make him fretful too. Or if the mood in the room is charged with tension from a shouting match on a drama on the television this will communicate itself to the baby or child too. Calm, quiet times before bed set the atmosphere perfectly. The less fuss and friction the better.

If things are tricky at bedtime and the child just won't settle it's sometimes helpful to also ask yourself; what is the pay-off for my child staying awake? For example, do they get another drink? Another cuddle? Another chunk of mum's time trying to settle them down? It's an easy scenario to fall into – a harder one to spot. Try and take away the pay-off.

Another pattern some mums find helpful is to establish a routine of allowing the child to fall asleep on their own and if they can't sleep then it's up to them to amuse themselves. For a baby this might be with the help of a mobile, or music or nightlights etc. For an older child a story tape, picture book, anything where they remain in bed – not playing where they're out of it. Grit your teeth and be firm, encouraging them to go to sleep on their own. This also gives the message that it is safe to do so, they are safe, you trust them to be able to do so.

Other mums feel it's far nicer for the baby to fall asleep on them and to keep their baby close throughout the night. It is completely up to your family.

Sometimes, if you get to desperation point and need some space from your baby in order to rest yourself, there may come a time when you have to leave them to bawl it out. In fact some babies do naturally cry themselves to sleep.

<u>A little story</u>

Although my general rule had been never to let my baby cry herself to sleep it got to the point where I felt so manipulated and resentful I did just that.

She had been ill, one of those intense times when you worry so much all routines go out of the window and I'd given in to every demand and kept her in bed with me as it was the only way to comfort her and get some sleep too. When it got to weaning her off those demands she wasn't so keen.

Six months later she was still screaming for attention every time I put her down and wasn't going to give that up for eight hour stretches of sleep all on her own. I began to feel that this was doing neither of us any good.

It took an awful lot of sobbing (her and me) and teeth gritting (me and her dad) and determination to get our happy bedtime routine back. But it was worth it because none of us was sleeping well enough to be a happy family during the day.

Amazingly, despite leaving her to sob angrily in her cot before she went to sleep I was amazed next morning when she greeted me with that wonderful smile. I was thinking she'd never love me again!

So whatever routine you get established it will change, and you can change it. The most important thing is to remain flexible and keep an eye on what *you're* doing and consequently what messages you're giving the child.

It helps to remember:

- The calmer you are, the calmer the baby/child will be.
- Try not to inadvertently give your child reasons to stay awake – like your attention. Even getting cross at them is attention.
- Create a calm and contented atmosphere leading up to sleep time.
- Be mindful of the fact that many programmes and media games have an enormous amount of tension in them that will affect babies and children even though they may not actually be watching them.
- Tension from these programmes and computer games affect the adults too which also passes to the children.
- Be boring.
- Be firm about your knocking off time.
- Try and be relaxed about it – going to bed is something for everyone to look forward to.
- Set a pattern that becomes familiar in the lead up to bed time and try and be consistent with it.
- Saying that don't be so obsessed that the baby can't sleep if something is missing.
- Make it happy, pleasant, enjoyable, loving.
- Do what suits your family best, not what necessarily suits everyone else.
- Be prepared to be flexible at certain times like times of illness; you will be able to change back if you need to. I just forgot to.
- Be patient. It changes. It's over so quickly.

Chapter Three

The Emotion Ocean

How are you feeling today?

Are you joyful or desperate? Calm or worried? In control or completely floundering?

Whatever they are, your feelings are a big issue. They can govern your day. They can be the catalyst for coping or not coping – that's how it is with motherhood for many mums.

Coping with motherhood is often more to do with managing your feelings than it is to do with anything practical. If you feel okay, you can usually cope with anything. If you don't, it's a struggle. That's why we need to pay attention to our feelings and find ways of understanding and managing them.

Hopefully, this chapter will help you on the road to doing that.

Feelings take some working out. They seem to do the most confusing things to you when you become a mother. They certainly don't seem programmed to help most of the time. Mostly, for quite some time after the birth, we feel overawed, exhausted, anxious, tearful, sudden ecstasy then the utter pits, so completely changed and inexplicably *something*. And if you are anything like me and my friends were you won't know quite what that something is. Not only that your feelings yo-yo so fast you just come to terms with them then they've swung the other way.

Be reassured; *this is perfectly normal*. This is how it is for lots of mums.

Almost every new mum goes through this. Many old mums go through it too, some at various stages of their mumhood life – it's not just you. In fact most mums have to deal with such different and challenging feelings about themselves, their baby, and their new life right from before the birth, during the birth, and often for a long time afterwards. This is what motherhood does to you. It is absolutely normal. Don't worry – it changes.

A little story

The first few days with that first new baby was a time I discovered that I could feel intense unimaginable joy. I could also feel disbelief, total uncertainty, absolute terror and ecstatic happiness all within a single ten minutes.

One dose of happiness that will stay with me forever; the first few moments when I'd become a mum. I remember looking down at her the first time I was alone and feeling absolute awe.

She lay cosseted in her shawl in the crux of my arm as I lay in bed slightly on my side to get a better view. Her nose was tiny. Her pink wrinkly fingers exquisite. Her hair dark and damp. Her eyes tight shut.

She smelt strange – not a smell I'd smelt before. One of warm skin and dry towels; uniquely scented with that slightly personal baby smell that each new human being has. My baby smell. Magic!

Her skin was like peony petals to touch, but warm. Her hair like the down on a peach. It was unbelievable.

It was the kind of feeling that rarely comes to you as an adult because you rarely get those kind of surprises any more. Like those surprises you had as a child when you opened a present and it was even better than you hoped for. A high not often paralleled. She was here. I could not stop staring. Happy. Replete.

I got home. Over the next few months I was confronted with the practicalities. I embarked upon the reality of life as a mum. And very soon the purity of that happiness vanished along with the purity of the pristine new babygrows. The reality of life at home with small children slapped me in the face.

Now I know that not every mum has that overwhelming awe and happiness when they first see their baby. It is a *completely* different experience for everyone. But what most of us do experience is an upsurge of feelings and emotions that we didn't expect and couldn't have predicted. And that's often the hardest thing to deal with. Being unpredictable there is no way you can prepare.

Support with initial feelings

I'm glad to be able to tell you that I and my mum friends, who all experienced such an emotional eruption, soon grew a different kind of happiness. Once we levelled out a bit.

It took a while to grow. Much went on to get there. And I learned lots of different lessons about managing the way you feel as a mum. But it would have been so much easier if I'd had some of the understanding that I have now back then. So much easier if I could have learnt all those lessons fast-track.

Here are some of those lessons. They are not black and white answers. They won't work for everyone all of the time. But it might help to have them to think about before we talk any more about emotions:

Thinking about emotions:

- *Your feelings are important* – you don't have to crush them, keep them hidden, bottle things up or feel guilty. Instead, listen to them, they're telling you something.
- *It's okay to be emotional* – being emotional at this time is natural. Your hormonal imbalance contributes to this state. Your emotions will even out in time. But until they do, better out than in, happy or sad ones, talk about them.
- *You are not the only mum to feel like this* – all mums suffer emotional upheavals. Yes, even the ones keeping it hidden. You're one of a crowd, welcome to the club.
- *You are perfectly normal* – every mum goes through feelings of turmoil, feelings of not being able to cope, terror, panic, fear, desperation, depression, uselessness. Being happy, then ten seconds later confusingly in tears. It's all normal.
- *You are a good mum* – a deeply feeling emotional mum is *not* a mum who is a pathetic wreck despite what you think. Being aware of your feelings is the first positive step towards understanding them. Once you understand them you can manage them. Understanding your feelings will enable you to help your children with theirs and you'll be doing a good job as a mum if you can do that.
- *You are coping* – coping doesn't necessarily mean coping all the time. I had times of not coping. My friends had times of not coping. We help each other out. We all cope in the end. Our children are not scarred for life by a few times of not coping. Relax.
- *Feeling wretched* - feeling you wish you weren't a mum sometimes, doesn't mean that you don't love your child, or you're not going to be a good parent. It gets to us all like that sometimes. Motherhood does make you feel wretched

sometimes, all things in life make you feel wretched sometimes, but it makes you feel tremendous sometimes too.
- *Crying is allowed* – crying is normal. Don't be ashamed if you cry. Motherhood can be upsetting. Nurture yourself better as you would your child. Then move on.
- *Talking about your feelings with other mums really helps* – it's such a relief when you screw up courage to tell another mum how wretched you feel sometimes to discover she feels exactly the same way. A good mum friend to share your feelings with is such a help. A mum who doesn't admit her feelings to you or belittles yours is not such a helpful friend to have. Opening up to other mums helps keep your feelings in perspective and it will help other mums too. It broadcasts the fact that feelings are just a natural part of adjusting to being a mum and that will make it all so much easier to bear. Don't forget to talk about the nice feelings too.
- *All these feelings will pass* – they're just like clouds on a blue sky. They blot the sun for a while, but it's always bright underneath and clarity will return. Trust. If you are absolutely swamped at times a simple distraction can sometimes ease overwhelming intense feeling – something like putting the telly on, connecting online, going out for a walk, taking a bath, contacting someone and making a date to meet, reading a magazine, getting some exercise.
- *Don't be afraid to seek help* – we all need help at times. I did. My friends did. Help from friends, relatives, midwives, nurses, doctors. If it gets bad to seek help is not giving in it is taking a positive, effective step towards changing it, which can only be good. In fact, seek help whether it gets bad or not. In no other job would you be expected to operate without help and guidance, without an induction. Asking others is like your induction. Use others' experiences and give them the pleasure of helping out.

Sometimes, some mums feel alright at the start, then your feelings seem to go downhill from there – this can even happen a year later. Because it's often a little way into motherhood that you get your wake up call. You get your biggest most overwhelming feeling when, like for me, the reality sets in. The attention, the gifts, the visitors, all suddenly stop and you're on your own. The joy, the celebration and the sheer wonderment of the miracle of the new baby carries you along on top of the surf for a while. But for many mums the surf board is soon whipped away and you drop into the ocean of reality with the sudden realisation that: *You're* *a mother now, not just for now but **for ever after**, how on earth are you going to cope with that?*

That's a mightily daunting thought.

Be reassured, you can handle it, you do find a way, every mum has to go through a period of adjustment. Remember, it's no small thing that you've done, it's *life-changing*. You're not going to adapt to it without some upheaval. And what you need to cope with is not only managing the practicalities of looking after a baby or child, it is also managing how you feel about that now you truly see the reality of this life changing work you now need to do.

<u>A little story</u>

My friends and I talked a lot about the feeling of being overwhelmed, about feeling unable to cope, about wanting to hand the baby back now we knew what motherhood entailed.

We talked about never managing to measure up to the images of The Perfect Mother who always had home made biscuits to pass round, a baby with never a speck of goo on it and a toddler without grubby dungarees like ours had.

But we also talked about the wonderful things too. The sheer all-consuming joy of holding our child. Of that soft cuddly body curled so neatly on our laps. Of those arms just the right size to fit round our necks. A downy head under your chin.

And what we see now is those sweet moments all gone. This is both sad and reassuring because just as the gorgeous bits go – the tricky hard bits go too. It all changes.

Our children are grown up now. They can stand on their own feet and put their cheek to mine. They don't fit on my knee, not that it stops them sitting on it! And we talk together adult to adult, which is what they are now. And my friends and I agree we wouldn't have wanted to miss it for the world.

So we wanted to remind you to be careful not to forget to enjoy the sweet moments because you are dwelling too much on the tricky moments. For just like the sweet moments, the tricky moments race past *too. A comforting thought – keep that in mind when the challenges feel never ending.*

One of the most immediate and effective ways to cope with overwhelming feelings, particularly the grim ones, which is also part of looking after yourself, is to *relax*.

Relax

Now, I was never very good at that. It was something I really had to work at. But by just relaxing all the intensity is taken out of everything.

If you relax then your child relaxes. If your child relaxes it helps you relax even more, it's a magic circle. If you relax then the atmosphere changes too, everything feels so much better, even though there may be no physical differences in what you're doing. When you are relaxed problems never seem half so bad. In fact in a relaxed state of mind is often when clarity strikes and you can see solutions. You can sometimes even look back over situations and wonder what you were in such a stew about.

Some mums find it very difficult to relax, particularly at the start when you feel so conscientious about your new motherhood. Some mums never manage to give themselves *permission* to relax. They like to be seen to be busy all the time, which is a shame, perhaps something we need to think about in the chapters ahead.

Sometimes though, the inability to relax is a sign of being over tired, overwhelmed, or needing to look after yourself a little better.

Relaxation is a vital skill, one you will need to turn to throughout the challenging times of being a parent if you are going to be able to sustain doing it well. Not only that, relaxation is also a valuable skill you will be able to pass onto your child, a valuable tool for their life too.

Sometimes you really do have to let go; allow others to help, take some time. But some quick methods that help when you're getting near breaking point, which you can do even with your baby there are:

- Five deep breaths – sometimes we breathe so shallowly on a daily basis.
- Stopping and counting to ten, twenty, fifty – you can do this while you breathe perhaps.
- Using some relaxing or uplifting music.
- Watching a relaxing programme or social networking.
- Reading or looking at a magazine.
- Going outside or into another room sometimes.
- Doing an activity you find enjoyable.

- Just being still and aware; enjoying a flower, lighting a candle, smelling some perfume or essential oil, rubbing your neck, eating an apple and being mindful of the flavour, stretching.

There are many relaxation books and tapes and meditation guides available that detail methods that you may find helpful. Use them when you have help around and time to yourself to practise some of the more detailed techniques.

Having said all that, it is really difficult sometimes because to relax we have to let go of the way we feel.

The thing that helps us to manage to do that better is to think about what influences the way we feel and therefore begin to understand *why* we feel as we do. Sometimes it isn't what we think it is. If we understand the reasons for the way we feel it somehow doesn't seem so bad, and at least we have some chance of managing better and making changes if need be, whether it's practical, mental or spiritual.

Looking at some of the things that influence our emotions

Looking at the things that can affect our emotions when we become mums they seem to fall into two groups. The first group is made up of immediate circumstances that happen straight away. The second group contains more long term things that can happen over a period of time.

Things that have immediate impact

Our first feelings are often floods of topsy-turvy, inherent emotions, some completely inexplicable and often out of proportion but very real. These rapid flooding feelings are often fast-changing, influenced by things that are happening *right now*, whipped up by your current circumstances like an endlessly crying baby, or everything going wrong when you're changing the nappy, etc. Not to mention fluctuating hormone levels. Some of them are immediately solvable and often short-lived.

These feelings are affected by immediate circumstances like:

- Your physical state after the birth,
- How much support you receive,
- How much rest you're able to get,
- These two of course affect how tired you are which affects everything,

- How you feel about your baby,
- What sort of person you are – how flexible and adaptable, a naturally calm person or an inherent worrier,
- How you manage the practicalities.

Some of these we'll think about in a minute. First let's look at the other group.

Things that affect us over longer periods of time

These are the feelings that are often affected by outside influences; often social, cultural or political even. Things like our relationships with family, friends or peer groups which sometimes change when we become mums, our profound ideas about our life as a mum, our expectations, external pressures, judgements and expectations from others. Feelings deep down we may not even be aware of that are influencing us but which take more thinking out and have bigger implications.

These feelings are affected by broader issues than the first group. Things like:

- How you manage this new job of being a mum,
- How you see your role as a mum (different from job),
- Expectations; yours and others,
- How you rate the value of what you do as a mum,
- Your relationship with your growing child,
- Finding happiness in your life as a mum who is another person too.

These issues are deep and complicated and take some thinking out. They are issues that affect our feelings over a longer period of time, without us even being aware of them, as we rarely give them consideration except perhaps in hindsight much later in our mumhood. Then we suddenly realise we feel really wretched about everything and not know why. Often it's because we haven't *thought* through these issues for ourselves, because it is actually our *thinking patterns* that affect the way we feel more than anything else. And if we fall into a negative thinking pattern, often as the result of what everyone else is telling us to think, it can be very destructive.

So I'd like to think those issues through individually in the following chapters. Right now though, I'd like to think about some of the more immediate influences from the first group that happen right at the start of motherhood.

Recovery, rest, support and tiredness and the effect they have on the way you feel

The first four come under the same umbrella. They are all linked and influenced by each other.

Recovery from the birth, getting rest and receiving support will all affect how tired you feel. I know we spoke about it in chapter two but it's so important to understand just how much tiredness affects our emotions. Tiredness can create feelings of despair, inability to cope, stress and overwhelm. And if you remember all you've been through, sleep deprivation included, you're bound to feel tired. When you are tired it is very hard to keep your thoughts positive and if your thoughts are not positive then neither will your feelings be.

One of the things I hear mums say to their toddlers a lot is 'don't cry darling, you're just tired'. Yet we often forget the simple blatant truth; the same goes for us too. *Tiredness affects us in the same way.*

Here are some of the ways:

- Tiredness makes us emotional, but that's often overlooked.
- Tiredness can reduce us to quivering heaps who don't feel able to function.
- It makes us unable to do the simplest of things and the worse it gets the more in denial we become.
- Tiredness will make you feel you're not coping as a mum, when the truth is you're just not coping *at the moment* and this moment will change.
- Tiredness can make the smallest of jobs look mountainously overwhelming.
- Tiredness contributes to feelings of stress and depression.

So if you're feeling overwhelmed, stressed, down and tearful one way of addressing it is to ask yourself these questions:

1) Am I simply tired?
2) Am I getting enough rest?
3) Can I find more support?
4) Who can I ask to babysit for a while?

5) How can I schedule my day so I get some rest?
6) What simple changes can I make so I feel less tired? (A change is as good as a rest).
7) What are the important jobs and what jobs can wait?
8) What really matters to me most?

Another point about tiredness is that it is deceiving in that it can *mask* itself for what it is.

<u>A little story</u>

My mother always used to say to me 'I can always tell when you're tired, dear, for the more tired you are the faster you go'. Infuriatingly she was right. The more tired we feel the more we do to pretend we're not. I could see it in my youngest too, the more tired she was the more like a tornado she became.

So, even if you don't want to admit it, accept that if you're feeling down right now it *might* be a result of tiredness and try and work out ways to help yourself overcome it. Use your strategies of looking after yourself. Ask for help. It would be a shame if you were less of a mum than you wanted to be to your child simply because you didn't ask for a little help when there are probably people around you who would love to do so.

Remember what we discussed at the start because it all affects your feelings; give yourself a recovery period, look after yourself and rest when you can. If there's truly no one around to help just prioritise the important things and forget the other stuff for now. Put your concern on hold – see how it looks in the morning. Keep a variety of special things aside that entertain your child so you can use them to keep them occupied when you need to rest.

By using strategies to help keep you rested at least it won't be deep tiredness that's impacting on your emotions, even if a little. And you will be able to enjoy your mumhood more and actually be a much better parent. For a rested parent is a parent who parents far better than a ratty one. And a rested parent also feels completely different about their child than a tired one.

How you feel about your baby, how you feel about your child

One of the things that can send mums' feelings into emotional overdrive is the way they feel about their child. It's a bit like starting a whole new relationship.

When you're fresh into a new relationship with a boyfriend or partner there's always the possibility of losing it, of course, but because you're in love you can't see that happening and you have no fears; you feel safe, enveloped in it, as if you could walk on water, on top of the world.

The love between mums and babies and children is nothing like that. Nothing prepares you for it. It is intense, it can be a love that fills you up to bursting, but also makes you feel extremely vulnerable or afraid, and often hugely anxious about the enormity of the responsibility.

And the love between a mother and child is *completely different for everyone.*

It can be totally non-existent. It can be all you need. It can make you feel so complete you wonder how you're ever going to love your partner any more. It can make you feel scared. You can feel absolutely nothing at all for your baby. You can feel numb. You can feel vulnerable. You can feel like you have no control any more. You can feel terrible guilt. You can feel so overawed and consumed with possessiveness you wonder how you will survive it.

Feelings for your baby can be both a blessing and a burden. These emotions are all normal. And they come and go. Remember; we're all different. Most important of all; *nature has a hand in it.*

Bonding

Bonding with your child is something that's talked about a lot by midwives and health workers until it gets to the point where you feel it's something you're going to be tested on! But how you bond – if at all – with your baby is entirely *individual to you* and that's how it should be. It's part of your genetic make-up, your personality, your characteristics – all the things that nature has given you. Nature makes you respond to circumstances in your own special way, nature is what partly determines the love you feel. Sometimes you can change this. Sometimes you can't. Sometimes there's no need to. You are an individual mum, as all mums are. Just be who you want to be.

It's also only *your* business, no one else's. Never think you *should* feel a bond others are feeling. Never feel you *should* be connecting or loving in the way everyone else is. Your relationship with your child is *up to you and what nature determines for you.*

Some mums feel complete adoration straight away. Some don't. Some grow a different kind of love over time. There is no right or wrong way to love. As long as you are demonstrating affection and care in your own special way then you are doing it right.

Immediate feelings for a new baby change over time. Whatever was felt at the start all mums report a different kind of love as their child grows. Your relationship with your child changes all the time, because your baby and child change all the time. That's why it helps to remain flexible; allow what you feel to be open to change. What can be difficult sometimes is coping with the feelings you have, whatever they are like, because they can be so powerful.

A powerful attachment to your baby can make you feel so scared of losing them or anything happening to them. You can feel vulnerable to hurt through their hurt, pained by their pain and all this can make it difficult to hand the baby over to someone else so you can get a break or a rest perhaps. It can make you feel guilty for doing so. It certainly makes you worry.

Equally you can feel guilty for being *keen* to take every opportunity to hand her over. Or not loving your baby in the way others seem to, for not feeling what others describe, or being with it one hundred percent of the time.

Being keen to get a break has nothing to do with how much you love your child or not, it's about doing what fits for you, what keeps you fit to be a good mum to it.

Also, the child has a hand in it. Just as it is important to remember that all mums are different, it is also important to remember that *all babies and children are different too.*

Babies are not all equal

An easy, sleepy baby who seems to be no bother, has plenty of naps, never cries and lies contentedly all day is extremely easy to care for, so some mums get plenty of respite naturally and can spend longer with their baby without the need for others' support.

A restless colicky baby who cries incessantly, who feeds incessantly, who never sleeps for any length of time and needs constant carrying about, is going to make any mum feel entirely different from the first example. Stress and tiredness can affect what we feel for our baby as much as it affects all our feelings. A mum with a demanding baby like this will need lots of support. A baby like this makes it much more difficult for mums to cope.

An easy, biddable child who seems to understand and respond appropriately to social cues right from the first telling can induce completely different feelings in a mum than a demanding, aggressive, hyperactive one who is never still for a minute.

Now, I know we're supposed to love our babies and children all the same. But they are not the same, and that does make a difference. It makes a difference to the way we feel. It is difficult to love them all the same when they have their unique idiosyncrasies some of which are particularly demanding. You have to find the right way for you to love your individual.

A unique and individual feeling grows for each of our unique and individual children, different for each. But it takes time to grow. It takes time to build up this relationship with them. And time will often sort it out.

If it doesn't and what you feel is causing you concern, again, it is so helpful to talk to someone about it. Friends, health visitor, doctor. It is far better to air your concerns, to let them out, than to bottle them up and go on struggling with overwhelming feelings. What you don't want to do is to feel guilty – in other words treat yourself badly – for not feeling the same about your child as the other mums you know. Keep reminding yourself that everyone is different, both mums and children. Mums who have not experienced a demanding baby will think their baby's good because they're perfect parents. Mums who have know the reality – they know it's not just the parenting it's the nature of the baby too.

<u>A little story</u>

I can remember times of thinking that I didn't love my child. There are times even now when it is easy to lose sight of the love we all feel for each other in this family when it becomes buried under every day stresses and strains, when everyone just seems to argue, when we all seem at loggerheads. But that happens in all families and it's usually only surface stuff. I know that deep down we all love each other dearly, it's just that life gets in the way sometimes. Underneath we have a strong, unique bond – I see this in the way that our kids, at times inclined to bitch at each other, now have a very intense loyalty and would do anything to support the other. It's lovely to witness.

I recognise this now. And I also know what helps. It helps to:

- Slow down.
- Put life aside.
- Make time for the loving bits.

Sometimes you think there are no loving bits, it's all slog. But there probably are if you think about it. Here are some ideas which might help:

Thinking about the loving bits:

- Try looking at them when they are asleep.
- Have a nap together side by side.
- Get your child giggling.
- Stop fussing over 'perfect' and enjoy playing with them whatever age they are.
- Don't worry about having a clean, tidy house all the time.
- Do things together. Get involved at their level.
- Slow down. Change nappies slowly, take time over feeding, stop chivvying. Just take more time. Children and babies need time taking. If your schedule seems too tight perhaps you need to make some changes.
- Go for a walk together. Rhythmic walking calms you both down. Enjoy showing your child the world.
- Watch a film together.
- Just sit and caress their hair or rub them gently as if you would stroke a cat.
- Talk about how you're feeling to others.
- Keep taking breaks. It's true that absence makes the heart grow fonder.
- Remember that all mums love differently. Look to the way you want to love.
- Also remember that all children are different in their demands and this can affect how you feel towards them. Be patient with yourself as much as your child.
- Finally, remember it all changes very quickly.

Of course, the feelings you have for your child do have longer-term implications on your relationships, so we'll return to them throughout. Right now, try and just take time to get to know them, take time to enjoy being their mum, enjoy the bits you like and try not to think too hard about the other bits, and allow yourself to relax with your child. There is nothing more important that you could be doing other than building this relationship which will become the basis of your parenting. Try and trust that over time you will be able to resolve any concerns you have.

What sort of person are you?

As I said earlier, nature has a hand in how you feel. The type of person you are affects the feelings you have, the types of feelings you have, how strong they are and how you cope with them.

Some mums seem to have personality types that are well suited to motherhood. They are calm and relaxed, they don't get stressed easily, they don't worry unnecessarily, they manage all that's thrown at them with ease, keep their emotions in equilibrium and cope with it as easily as sailing on a smooth sea.

Unluckily for me, I wasn't one of them. I floundered about in a heaving emotion ocean, pitching about like a tiny vulnerable boat at the mercy of swelling tides.

A little story

I'm a terrible worrier. I fretted buckets over my babies and children. But it got to the point where I suddenly thought; hey, it doesn't have to be like this. Why don't I learn to respond to situations differently? Can I choose? Can I change my behaviour?

I discovered that I could...

Be aware of what you're like

Being aware of what you are doing, how you are responding to the challenges thrown at you, is a helpful strategy to managing your feelings rather than just being at the mercy of them. If we want to change the way we're feeling, the first step is to notice what triggers particular feelings within us. Most particularly *notice the way we're thinking*.

The power of thought is enormous – you only have to think hard about sucking on lemons and you get a reaction in your mouth. Our imaginations can create powerful reactions in us and our imaginations are powered by our thoughts. Our worries are powered by our thoughts. And thoughts we *can* change.

For example, some of us have vivid imaginations which go into overdrive about little things if we let them. Once we start worrying, we can make up scenarios in our mind of all the terrible things that could happen. Like if your baby is a bit restless and whiny you can begin to imagine they have something terribly wrong with them, or some awful illness. This makes you feel anxious and stressed and all the other feelings evoked by worry which transfers itself to the baby which exacerbates the situation. While the *real* situation might simply be that they are over tired and a quick soothing cuddle by a relaxed mum puts them to sleep.

The feelings our imaginations can evoke within us can be as real as if what we imagined was actually happening. And then we forget to be aware that this was *only* our imagination and we don't *have* to feel this way.

By being *self-aware* you can observe the way you respond to certain situations, think whether it's an appropriate response, and if it's making you feel awful, whether you need to respond that way anyway. Could you respond differently with your thinking? Think; 'I'll just be relaxed about this and see what happens'. This way you may find your responses can be changed.

Many of us give an unnecessary stress response to things that happen, often even really insignificant things that are easily rectified like a leaky nappy for example. In the broader picture what does a leaky nappy really matter? We're not going to die from it, for heaven's sake! We could instead just shrug it off and get on with the practicalities of dealing with it. Sometimes the way we react you'd think the world was coming to an end. Practical *action* often helps override unnecessary, stressful thoughts.

Being aware of the responses we make will give us the opportunity to make choices in our response and help us to handle things better, to respond perhaps in a more calm way. A calmer response will help to keep our feelings in proportion. Proportionate feelings are better than those that are way out of perspective. Responding disproportionately to situations is often a sign we're tired, may need more breaks, or a little more support.

Another aspect of our personalities, which has an effect on our feelings, is our ability to be flexible.

Try being flexible

The schedule of a mum's day changes unpredictably all the time; like the leaky nappy example – usually when you're just rushing out the door. Keeping flexible, not getting upset when things don't go according to plan, dealing with unexpected events with adaptability, watching your responses to changes of plan, helps you to cope in a calmer way than getting immediately up tight every time plans change. Dealing with the unexpected in a light hearted way is a key skill to an easier motherhood.

The trouble is some of us are not flexible, adaptable or light hearted. Flexibility doesn't always come naturally; some of us are up-tight people. This can make motherhood and all the unexpected things that come your way during the day, very stressful. But we don't actually have to stay like that. It is possible to make changes, people do achieve it.

Sometimes that up-tight approach to life is the result of a challenging work schedule we've been used to operating before we became mums. So it is one we learnt. And having learnt it, we could learn differently if we wanted to.

Learning to be more flexible takes concentration and practice. But it definitely helps if you want to be a calm, contented mum. Becoming more flexible is about letting go of what you *expected* to happen and accepting what *is* happening and applying yourself to the practical task of dealing with it. Instead of mourning over what hasn't happened; get *focussed* on what is happening right now. Change your thinking, change your functioning, change your old working habits to habits more in tune with your mothering.

Change old habits

Sometimes our old working habits are not very in tune with the habits we need to adopt to be a good mum. Some of those habits may well be things like being driven, meeting pre-set targets, being tough and getting on. These habits don't sit well with what's required of a mum. Mums actually need to adapt to a softer way of working, where sometimes it's impossible to get on, where we don't have to meet targets but need to go with the flow for a while and we don't have to be tough.

Not being tough or achieving our schedule for the day does not mean we are being weak. It takes a very strong person to soften their familiar character traits to meet the needs of their new circumstances. It takes a strong character to let go of old habits and strive to adopt new ones. It takes a strong character to understand that they don't have to achieve targets just to prove themselves to others. And a special kind of person to realise that motherhood is not about *getting* it is about *being*. It is about being on a journey you and your child are making, not about an outcome or impressing anybody.

It is a time when we do not need our tough workday characteristics, instead we need to use our softer caring characteristics in order to do this *new job well*. Our young children and babies do not need targets met. They need a good mum. Allowing yourself time to be aware of your intuitive, nurturing side at this time of your life is not about letting yourself go it's about adapting your skills to suit the job in hand now.

Besides, children don't need future targets met as much as they need to *live in the now*, be nurtured *now*, be cared for and attended to *now*. What you do now impacts on them later. And this time in their lives does not ever come again. It would be a shame to miss it by being too busy forward looking, or consumed with emotions that prevent us from enjoying it.

Being self-aware helps to stop that happening. Being aware of what sort of person you are will help you to make even little changes which will affect the way you feel and the way you enjoy your motherhood.

Let's think about that a minute:

Thinking about what sort of person you are:

- Are you calm? Calm makes for an easier ride through motherhood. If you're not naturally calm you could learn some calming and relaxing techniques.
- Can you relax? Keeping relaxed helps deal with many issues and ride out concerns. There are many books which might help you, not only about relaxation but other self help techniques too.
- Are you flexible? Life changes all the time while you're a mum. Notice whether this causes you extra stress – some people become very stressed when unexpected changes are thrown at them. Tell yourself these small things don't matter. Be adaptable and go with the flow of changes.
- Are you a perfectionist? Women who require everything to be absolutely perfect immediately put themselves under pressure

which causes stress. Mothering is never perfect. Try letting go of perfect and being content with things as they are.
- What causes you to be stressed? Try and identify little things that stress you out the most. Ask; do they really matter? Can you alter anything to make it better or can you alter your responses?
- Are you a bottler? Bottling feelings up is no way to deal with them. Be brave and try and talk about them. Most particularly your fears – we all have them.
- Do you have a racing imagination? Notice whether the things that stress you out are real or imaginary. Some people put themselves under extra stress by always imagining the worst scenarios. Don't pay attention to things that haven't happened.
- Can you get things out of proportion? This is often what our imaginations do to us. It seems doubly worse with motherhood. Talking to other mums, seeing what they do and learning from that often helps keep things in proportion.
- What kind of thoughts do you think? Are you basically a positive thinker or more the kind of person who only dwells on the negative things? You can spot this by noticing whether you moan a lot – that's negative thinking for you. Try and see the good side of things.
- Are you too competitive? Some mums act like it's a competition between us all to have the best baby, be the most attentive, be the best mum. This doesn't help mums and it certainly doesn't help us raise a happy healthy child. Try and steer clear of it.
- Are you still operating with your working persona? You may find that you need to adopt a different persona when you become a mum, operating at your softer and most caring best.

Being aware of these things, of the way we are, the responses we make, our thinking patterns, our habits and traits, is the first step to managing our feelings rather than have our feelings managing us.

It is not about having perfect characters or being perfect mothers. All of us have traits and characteristics that will be just right for motherhood yet which we might have had to keep hidden in the workplace or at other times in our lives. Now is the time to discover them and to use them to their best advantage. It is time to make the most of being the caring person you are – if you weren't caring you wouldn't be reading this book!

How you manage the practicalities and how that affects your feelings

There is a mountain of little practical jobs to manage when you become a mum. Many of us go through an enormous change of life style and it often includes being in the house more and having to pay attention to domestic type chores that are not that enjoyable. But actually, what you do to manage them often doesn't have as big an impact on you as how you feel about them.

The basic jobs you'll need to deal with every day may be little but they add up to a huge amount and you don't want to underestimate that, nor their impact. Things like; feeding, changing, sterilising, washing, cleaning, tidying, changing bedding, clearing up toys and equipment, more changing, trying to keep the house nice, never mind feeding or looking after you. There are so many little chores to attend to when you have a baby you wonder how you'll ever get dressed in a morning.

The unending toil of keeping on top of it all while your child grows can get mums down. Plus the fact that there's this growing infant who needs chunks of your time and attention as well. When all you had to pay attention to before was keeping the house tidy when no one was in it all day.

It is extremely overwhelming to be confronted by all the practicalities that need attending to once you are a mother. This is something all mums have to manage and cope with. It's something that my mum friends and I were really quite shocked about because none of them were included in our lifestyle before being mums and we had to adapt quickly. Here's something we learned;

<u>A little story</u>

Many of them don't matter. Not doing many of them doesn't make any difference in the end. Letting go of many of them; things like the tidying, keeping everything clean, putting things away etc, is far better than trying to maintain an order that is just not possible once kids are part of your life. And the real important job to be doing right now is loving your child and making the most of time you have to spend with them. More important than a tidy show home, gleaming surfaces, everything in its correct place.

One of my friends said that she is so glad she didn't miss that sweet time holding her child. The tidying didn't miss her attention, but her son certainly would have. You don't get a second go at it with children!

This is a time in our life when we just have to allow some of our attention to detail to be less important.

Work out what's important

Mumhood changes us. It changes our person, our personality, our daily lives. And it's no good people saying it doesn't because it does and it should. That's because we have a whole new dimension added to it, we are building a new relationship. Trying to keep it exactly as it was before motherhood happened to us denies the fact that there's a new being come into our universe and the way we raise that new being is *important*. Just as any new relationship or new experience changes us, becoming parents changes us too. And these changes require us to let go of the old as we adapt to the new.

As mums our life is completely new compared to what it was before we had a child. Our day to day jobs are new. Our roles are new. Our priorities will be new. Our values will need renewing. These new differences require us to rethink and grow and change.

These are the important issues that are going to be discussed in the following chapters where we will talk about our mumhood job some more. Because this new job affects us really deeply and *how much* it affects us is another aspect of motherhood that is often underestimated. These aspects are what affect our feelings long term. And affect the way in which we can enjoy our mumhood, not only now but also as a woman in the future.

For now though, there is some simple prioritising you can do:

- Pay attention to loving your child, to building this new relationship.
- Pay attention to looking after yourself.
- Do the bare essentials in the house so as to achieve the above.
- And don't worry about the rest at this time.

Prioritising will have an effect on the way you feel. Because trying to do all of the jobs all of the time will make you feel drained as it's well nigh impossible; there will always be something that needs doing. Prioritising and letting go can help make space in your day for you to value being a mum. That's perhaps the biggest priority of all.

Working out what's really important is discussed in the next chapter.

Tip-Bit No 3: Breast, Bottle and Bananas

Like the other tip-bits in this book, this one is not here to dictate to you what you should do or how you should do it when it comes to feeding your baby or child. It is just here to give you a few things to think about and to share a few tips that myself and other mums found useful. It's also here because the issue of breast feeding seems to be near the top of the list of things that raise mums' stress levels and feelings of anxiety.

This is so sad because breast feeding can be so easy and an exquisite joy. To some though it is a nightmare that they don't want to do, but often feel pressured into.

It doesn't need to be like this. So there are a few considerations that it might be helpful to start with:

a) You should only breast feed if it feels right for you
b) You don't have to breast feed if you don't want to
c) Give it a try and see how it feels but...
d) You don't have to feel guilty about the choices you make
e) You are not less of a mum if breastfeeding isn't for you

We seem to be a nation obsessed with food and feeding at the moment. One of the things mums told me when I was researching for this book was that breast feeding was the issue they found most difficult. It wasn't doing it, it was the way they were made to feel about it, especially those who didn't breast feed; they felt inadequate, humiliated, guilty.

Those who wanted to but couldn't manage it felt pathetic and useless. And many had their confidence and self esteem eroded by pushy professionals and relatives with little sensitivity and respect for privacy and individual choice and intuition.

It is sad to hear such stories. The start of our journey into motherhood can be tough enough without being made worse by this kind of pressure, especially at a time when we can feel so vulnerable.

When it comes to the way you feed your baby you will need to make your wishes clear and demand respect for your right to:

- Freedom of choice in the way you feed your baby.
- Respect for your decision.
- Privacy and lack of intervention in carrying out that choice.

- Support for your choice.

When you've just had a baby it's quite difficult to be strong if you are feeling overwhelmed, emotional and are recovering from the birth. So it's helpful to have thought this choice through beforehand and made your decision known to your partner or whoever will be supporting you.

It is a very personal issue and one which can be all consuming in the first few days after becoming a mum. Most mums feel like this and it helps to discuss the way you feel about it with others.

<u>A little story</u>

I wanted to try and breast feed. A few hours before coming home I tried my baby at the breast, but couldn't quite get going so the nurse interfered, shoving the baby's head at the breast as if trying to squash two balls together. The baby got distressed and wouldn't latch on. The nurse got cross and even suggested the baby was being 'naughty'. This didn't feel right to me.

Luckily for me I had this feeling deep down that we could do it if the baby and me had some time alone together. So I had a little practice later when no one was looking. Success! It was a lovely feeling.

Let me make it plain that most nurses are wonderful, caring, supportive people, which is exactly what new mums need. But this story shows that you should listen to your own intuition as well as to others.

Breast feeding is more about confidence in your ability as a mum, being relaxed, using your intuition, trial and error, than it is about particular technique really. There is no right or wrong way to do it; you have to do it the way that's right for you and the baby. It is a perfectly natural thing for you to be doing but, like with the birth, natural doesn't always make it easy.

It really is as natural a function as hugging and it feels lovely when it works, gives great opportunities for contact and can become something quite special between mother and child.

However, if it doesn't work for you then don't get stressed about it. It does have advantages; it's so easy when out, there's no messing around with bottles and sterilising etc, you have all you need to hand. The disadvantages are that you are tied to feeding or expressing, the father doesn't get a turn and misses out on this, and he also cannot help with night feeds.

Whichever route you choose it is over very quickly – I quite missed it when mine stopped. It is a lovely bonding time. But, despite the emotional blackmail some people use against mums it is important to know that *babies who are not breastfed are not scarred for life*. And *babies who are not breastfed are not loved any less*.

We are told that there is research to show that breast is best for babies. We are also told that the happiest babies, those that grow up into the happiest contented children, are those who have happy contented mums. Mums who have been forced into breast feeding or who have been made to feel bad about the way they feed their baby by external pressure are not contented mums. Therefore it makes sense to do what's best for you as the mum. Listen to your feelings and do what feels right.

If you want information about feeding your baby then research the baby info around. But do keep your intuitive instincts at the forefront of the information and listen to them too. Information and current theory changes regularly. Fads come and go. It's often best to go with gut feeling. It is your right to choose.

Whatever you decide you'll soon find it's moved on and you are into the next feeding stage; solids.

As I said earlier society seems to be obsessed with food and mums are no exception. It's another issue high on the stress stakes. But the most important thing you can do when you feed your infant is *not* to get stressed and obsessed with it. Keep it simple. Keep it calm. Be aware of your approach and your reactions. Don't panic about getting food into your child.

It helps to be aware of the fact that it is highly unlikely that any baby in this country is ever going to starve to death if they have a mum like you seeing to it. But it is more likely to refuse food if there is stress and anxiety surrounding feeding which could also develop difficulties later on.

Again, it is your choice what you feed your child and what routines you adopt. The overriding priority with any decision about what you feed your child is to do with nutrition.

Jars of baby food are fascinating and convenient but not really necessary and the contents often have the taste of cardboard and the consistency of slime – I wouldn't fancy it. They are also expensive and often have a mass of ingredients which are marketed as healthy, but then we've been told that all kinds of junk foods were healthy at one point too so I should be ever mindful of that.

Advertising techniques are also very good at suggesting our baby won't get all it needs if we don't feed them this commercial baby food, using its own brand of emotional blackmail to lure us in. But we don't have to buy into that. There is no reason why you cannot feed your baby the same nourishing food that you eat, mashed up, like vegetables and fruits, beans and casseroles, etc. But you will need to investigate your own diet and see whether it is healthy enough for your child and if it isn't maybe it's an opportunity for you to change. Apart from anything your baby will soon grow into an observant child and will be aware of what you are eating and that your bowl of chips appears to be far more appealing than the sludge that he's eating.

That aside, you will remember that in order for you to look after yourself well *you* need nourishing and valuable foods too for food can affect the way you're feeling as much as anything, especially if you have a diet high in sugar.

Eating well doesn't have to be complicated, in fact it's often the case the simpler it is the better. The nearer our food is to its natural state and the less processed and packaged it is the better. The more variety, both of type and colour we eat the better. We have to watch our salt and sugar content and of course fat. We need to see that the whole family is getting fruits and vegetables, proteins, carbs and fibre each day. These are the ways to manage feeding yourself in a nourishing and caring way. It matters; for your sake; for your child's sake.

The biggest effect on your child's diet and weight, not only now but for their future too, comes from your demonstration. So perhaps if you are not already, it is a good time for you to learn what's healthy and begin new habits.

It helps to also be aware, as you feed your children, that food affects their behaviour radically. Even some natural things do too so it's worth reading up on this particularly if you have a toddler who is a bit hyper. It's mostly processed foods and things like drinks and of course sweets that have the biggest impacts.

Children do develop fads and dislikes. It seems inevitable. But the less we make of them the better. And we need to keep offering foods even if they don't like them occasionally because their tastes change. Just because they don't eat bread early on in their life doesn't mean they won't eat it for life. So keep offering those fruits and vegetables and keep it varied and low key. Be flexible and adaptable and take care of yourself in your own eating habits too. This is the best way to set your child up for a healthy eating life.

Feeding doesn't have to be difficult, or a big issue. The less of an issue it is the better. Meal times just want to be happy, relaxed and easy. It doesn't matter too much about rules of where to eat, finishing every morsel, cutlery techniques. What matters is that it is a pleasant time. Each eating stage, and feeding fad, passes quickly and before you know it you'll be wondering how to keep your teenagers out of McDonalds every day. But then, if McDonalds isn't part of your life, it's less likely to be a big part of theirs either!

Chapter Four

Job Description

I'm going to do something now that I don't really want to do.

I'm going to look at being a mum as if it were a job; as if it were like any other employment you would have outside the home.

I don't like to do that because motherhood isn't the kind of job that can be fitted neatly into that kind of category – or any kind of category for that matter. Simply because it is a job that solely concerns *real live people* who are all wildly *different*. Who all bring something different to it. And it is exactly those *differences* that bring a quality to the job of being a mum that makes it so unique. It would damage the value of them to try and fit it into one description.

But a kind of job description for motherhood is useful. It will help you to recognise the job of being a mum for what it is.

What is a mum then?

But we all know what a mum is don't we? A mum is a person who has kids. Simple!

If only it were.

If I were to write a job description of a mum, I know the one I would have written starting out on this adventure of motherhood, when I was blindly naïve, would be wildly different from the one I would write now I have experienced it. Not to mention much shorter.

It probably would have gone something like this: Person required to look after baby/child; to change, feed and clothe, offer comfort and stimulation when appropriate. Duties give employee ample time to enjoy coffee mornings and other social activities with other mums, as well as shopping and other leisure pursuits. Thus allowing her to lead her other life as well as being a mum.

The more accurate job description...

Many years of being a mum and the job description I would write now would go something like this: Person required to undertake gruelling 24/7 duties to a baby/child. There will be no free time, no breaks, no holidays, no time off even overnight. Likely to entail complete loss of personal identity, social life, and generally life as it was before. Involves deprivation of sleep, energy, looks, figure, and mental and emotional health. Along with physical and emotional hardship. Entails enormous stress unlikely to have been experienced before. Not suited to the faint hearted or for those not used to multi-tasking, who are not flexible and adaptable or able to put their own needs aside.

It's not that I want to be pessimistic or anything, or to put you off. But much of that *is* what happens. It also happens that being a mum can be *the most wonderful, fulfilling, brilliant, joyous* job a woman is ever likely to have the good fortune to do.

Yet we often don't notice because of the shock and the change. And I'm making the point not because I want to be negative about it; no, it's just that I want to show you *how hard you work* as a mum because it's seldom acknowledged.

<u>A little story</u>

Whenever my mum friends and me got together to chat one of the most common topics that came up time and time again – after we'd talked about the babies till we were blue in the face of course – was the multitude of hidden jobs that being a mum entailed and we had never before credited mums with working so hard at. I'm quite ashamed to say that if we'd known how hard mums work we would perhaps have been much, much more respectful and understanding. I'm hoping that this book will help acknowledge and champion that.

How hard you work

To feel worthy in the work you do and go forward into being content with it you do need to *appreciate and acknowledge* how hard you work in becoming a mum.

Becoming a mum is a huge undertaking. It involves an enormous amount of labour. It has a hugely understated personal toll. And I mention all this not to put you off – but so that you can give yourself *credit*.

One of the hardest aspects of being a mum is perhaps not the intensity of the labour, or the millions of little integrated jobs you do all day long, it's the fact that you get *no credit* for having done them. And it's that which makes a difference to how you feel about it and in the end how much worth you attach to doing it.

Few people seem to recognise the fact that to be a mum you also have to undertake to be a nurse, doctor, teacher, cook, laundry maid, cleaner, home manager, personal assistant, chauffeur, secretary, referee, analyst, psychologist, director, actor, shoulder to cry on, poop-scooper, stand-by and back-up, climbing frame . . . I'd better stop, I'm getting carried away. I guess you'll see what I'm getting at.

You labour on, day after day, doing millions of little tasks. Like hunting for odd shoes, mopping messes off the floor, consoling tears and fights, wiping slippers of those who've just stood in the mess, taking the Duplo out of the potty, scrubbing the soaked in pee off the carpet, picking up toys, mending the ones you've just stood on. Tidying over and over again the tidying you've just done because the two year old whirlwind has just undone it. On and on you labour at all those little mini-jobs for which you get no recognition.

Labours like those in the workplace would be recognised and listed on a job description. If they weren't you'd be quite justified in not doing them.

But unlike with a job description *none of this work* was written down before you did this job of being a mother. You probably had no idea what you were letting yourself in for. Thus the workload comes as a bit of a shock.

Most of us have been lucky enough to be employed. We've mostly understood the job we've been about to take on. We know what's going to be expected of us. We start out, if nervous, at least from that understanding.

With motherhood it is *nothing* like that. There is *no* real understanding or appreciation beforehand of what it all entails.

Why is all this relevant?

Because it takes some adjusting to. Because no one is going to be happy in their work if that work is not recognised for what it is in the first place. And if you don't get credit or *give yourself credit* for it.

It's *so* important you recognise the *enormity* of the work you do to be a mum, right from the start. Only then will you see that it is completely understandable that you should sometimes feel overwhelmed with it. Anyone would. The job of being a mum is *huge*. Don't underestimate it.

Credit yourself with all that you do. Appreciate yourself. Hold your head up – *you work hard.*

All mothers work incredibly hard to achieve all that they do, all that is required to be done to *raise another human being.* Mums are an absolute champion workforce, incredible plate-spinners, and adept managers.

It is tough sometimes to be confronted with it all. But even worse: to be confronted with the fact that you get very little recognition for all the work you do, day after day, to be a good mum.

That is why mums have the hardest job in comparison to any other employment. And it wasn't long before my husband agreed with that.

A little story

My husband soon got to know that days at home with the children were far more demanding than his twelve-hour working days outside the home. After two days at home with the children he turned from that sweet, easy-going, young-looking father into a white, lined, stressed, Hitler figure who had difficulty being pleasant to anybody. He understands how hard mums work.

But society is very remiss at crediting women with that. If women complain about it, they get accused of nagging or whinging. If women just don't do it, they get accused of being unfit mums or Women's Libbers (in a detrimental tone). If mums just grin and bear it, they tend to become depressed, dull and downtrodden mums.

There is another way:

Recognise all you do

Understand that your work is of *extreme value.* I'd love to see mums giving themselves credit for the work they do. And not inhibit that credit by thinking that *their work is any less valuable because it's taking place in the home.*

Each and every mum needs to recognise that this job of being a mum includes a *labour that exceeds what you'd normally find in a work place, which alone can be enough.* For years and years we've credited physical labour, industrial labour and intellectual labour, all of which mums do. But what's missing from that list is emotional labour, something that mums toil at along with all the others.

Emotional labour, that is engaging with your baby and child and taking the time to attend to their development, part of which is emotional, has as big an influence on the world as all the others. Acknowledge and give yourself credit for that.

Some women rarely credit themselves with 'working' at all, if that work is looking after their children. Some women don't credit themselves with doing a job of work because that work happens to be inside the home and unpaid.

But in response to that I look at it this way: if a woman got the job of being a nanny to someone else's children, she would get credit for having employment – for doing valuable work, and credit for all the labour she would do in order to look after those children. Not to mention the prestige of getting paid. But if women devote time to being there to look after their *own* children they get no credit, or kudos, for doing a job of work at all. Yet it is exactly the same job.

Ironic isn't it?

Make sure that you are recognising the work you do to look after your child for what it is. Give yourself credit. For it is not the amount of the work that can steal away your sense of worth or happiness. It is the lack of credit you give yourself for doing it.

Hard work alone doesn't make for discontent. Lack of appreciation of it does.

Sometimes the work involved in looking after young children can be tedious, boring and repetitive, as can any job of work. But it only becomes unbearable when it stays unappreciated.

Be good to yourself. Appreciate that every little task is part of this larger job you now do. Credit yourself with how hard you work because if *you do* – so will everyone else, thus improving attitudes to all mums. So you will be establishing a sense of worth and credit in what mums do, for all mums not just for yourself, and gradually you may change attitudes. What a contribution that would be.

The conditions under which mums work

As if the amount of labour you do looking after your children wasn't enough I'm afraid there's something else that actually makes it worse; the conditions under which you do that work.

You see – this is another aspect of motherhood that is little appreciated or little accredited to the job of work you do to be a good mum to your own children; the difficult conditions under which you work.

Again – I'm not saying this to be negative. I always found being a mother to my babies brought me unparalleled joy. But that doesn't make it easy and I want you to acknowledge that.

This is where it helps again to look at mumhood as if it were any other job.

In any other job description you would expect the hours, the holidays, the demands, to be clearly stated as you would the duties. So you would know what conditions you were letting yourself in for.

This doesn't happen when you undertake the job of a mother. The conditions under which mums work tend to come as a bit of a shock.

For a start there are the hours. There's just no getting away from the fact that with small children you work twenty four hours out of twenty four, seven days a week. Even when you are asleep or they are asleep you are always 'on call'. Waiting. Ready to be there. Half listening. Tense. On duty. Always.

Once a mum always a mum. There's no going back. Those conditions come with the job. And they're extremely tough. You may also get the wonderful bonus of unconditional love but that doesn't make it any less tough.

It is also impossible to have a holiday in the sense that you knew it before. Your work now goes with you. There's no switching off. No getting away from it. Even handing your baby or child over to someone else doesn't ensure that you get a mental or emotional holiday away from all the worries and concerns that the work of being a mum brings. That's the way of it. It's not that you can't enjoy it and find great delight in being away with your baby, but it's worth understanding that the sense of 'holiday' has altered.

There are not even any real breaks in the day. Except snatched ones – unscheduled ones that you might get unexpectedly and can't be planned for or looked forward to. And you remain on-call anyway. That's why it's essential to take breaks when you can – to make up for it.

A little story

My partner would sometimes ring me in his lunch break. He was lucky - he got a lunch break. A whole hour off duty. His calm voice illustrated the relaxation he felt at that time. I was probably trying to feed a restless toddler while breast feeding the baby at the same time and trying to snatch a bite for myself. The last thing I needed to do right then was answer the phone to someone having a nice break in his working day. One which I wasn't getting!

We've talked about the amount of jobs involved. The conditions that make those jobs so much harder is the fact that they are not scheduled in the first place; you never know when they're going to be sprung on you, and you have to keep switching the agenda all the time, known to be stressful. The hardest thing of all – there's no induction day, no training, or no other helpful employee to guide you few those first moments with this new job.

It used to be family who would take on the role of supporting new mums through this difficult induction time. But families now are spread so far and wide across the country that there is no longer that kind of support. And I think it makes the job very hard for new mums. Many are really going it alone. Online networking is no replacement for having another pair of hands right there. And this is tough. These are the conditions under which you work. Acknowledge it.

Then, of course, there's the new boss to get used to.

The new boss (your baby)

Did you ever have a boss that made so many draining, unending, compulsory demands as your infant? I doubt it. Your new boss takes some getting used to. You have to decide when to comply with your boss's demands and when they're unreasonable and you need to resist. Your new boss completely overwhelms your life and expects you to give up your 'other' life to tend to him properly. He expects commitment in a big way and ties you to that commitment with a big emotional bond.

Not only that your new boss will expect that commitment now for *life*.

It is a few years into motherhood before the realisation of that commitment *really* hits. With most jobs, if you get a bit fed up or restless, or feel it's time to move on or move up, you can usually change your job. Make a fresh start. Go for promotion.

No chance of that with motherhood. I've enjoyed every stage of my job as a mum – every part of my relationships. But just occasionally the outlook of ongoing domestic needs can appear to be unchangingly tedious and monotonous. Some mums come to a sudden realisation that you're in a trap you're tied to forever. Not a happy feeling that.

Neither is the frustration that comes with never being able to do anything for longer than a few minutes without having to change to something else, to interrupt what you're doing, to abandon all plans and switch to something else. This is how motherhood goes most of the time. It can be a frustrating condition of your working day. Try and make small changes to help you handle these frustrations like sharing workload and child time with others or planning time away from it.

Multi-tasking

Multi-tasking might be recognised as a valuable skill but actually it is stressful. Yet it is something mothers have to do all the time to pull in all the demands on them during the day. Every mum will be familiar with the feeling of having to do several things at once. Having to feed a baby, answer a toddler's questions, prepare the toddler a drink too as he's not going to get left out, cook supper and just at that minute the phone blips as notifications come in. It's very stressful to work under conditions like this. And they are like this most of the time for most mums. That's what it's like – this job of being a mum.

All these demands take some getting used to. And despite the wonderful joy of your child it's very, very hard work that you do. That's why you need to give yourself credit for doing it. Understand that:

You are one of the most skilled and hardest working work forces in the world.

It is as hard a job as any full-time employment. In fact I think the conditions of the job make it far harder. The biggest condition is perhaps one that never gets a mention – the fact that at the end of the day it isn't even rewarded with *pay*!

BUT:

More good news

The good news is; it's rewarded in other ways. It *is* manageable. And it doesn't always have to be like this. Despite the hard work, despite the sometimes overwhelming conditions, motherhood is one of the most wonderful opportunities for you to learn and grow and develop personally, to imbue a sense of worth and being needed, to explore and discover parts of you which you never knew existed.

You are also in a role that has the potential to make an enormous difference and an enormous contribution to the world; you are a *parent!* Parenting is a life changing responsibility – and opportunity to involve yourself with something *great - for ever after.*(More on that later).

Understanding and crediting yourself with the work you do as a parent is a big step towards making it tolerable *longer term* – because it is a long term job - and being more content doing it, a step towards being a mum who is not resentful or overburdened. Nothing breeds resentment more than unexpected workload, unexpected conditions, no credit or appreciation of how hard it is.

But it isn't *all* hard toil. You *can* look at it differently. Before you do that here are a few things to think about:

Thinking about credit:

- Credit yourself with doing a hard job.
- Give yourself credit for the enormity of the workload.
- Give yourself credit for the hard conditions you work under.
- Understand that it is an overwhelming job and that it's normal to feel overwhelmed.
- Enjoy the loving bits as well as the work.
- *Look after yourself* as well as 'the boss'.

The most valuable job in the world

There is no doubt in my mind that the job of being a mum is *one of the most valuable* jobs that I've ever done.

It is also the hardest job I've ever done with the most demanding conditions.

Not only that but it's never completely understood until you have lived it. So that makes for quite a large proportion of society who are unwilling to recognise this job for what it is, and unlikely to give much needed support. That needs changing in society and your attitude towards your valuable job right now can help. Helps you cope too, with all the demands made on you.

Sometimes you can get so wrapped up in all the labour of those demands you can get it all out of proportion, you forget about the loving bits, and you get to the point where it's difficult to cope, let alone enjoy your child.

There are two things you can do to help you cope and to help you enjoy.

The first thing you can do is to ask yourself a very important question: *What exactly is my role now?*

This is a major issue. This is what governs what you do, the jobs you do, and how happy you are doing it. This is such a big issue I want to talk about it in depth in the next chapter. Perhaps you could be thinking about it while you do the second thing.

The second thing you need to do is to *change your point of view* about all those little jobs you're trying to get through in one day.

Rethink the labour. Prioritise. Decide what's important. Be prepared to *change your perspectives* - even if they are perspectives that you are desperate to cling on to.

Changing your perspectives on the home front

It is staggering to discover that when this one small being comes into your world it brings with it not one small amount of stuff. But a huge mountain of it. In fact a whole mountain range.

A range of accessories. A range of kit to clothe it in. A range of equipment to look after it. And an ENORMOUS amount of labour is required to keep on top of it all.

How can this one small being make such a massive disruption not only to your schedule, but also to the state of the house? The place soon becomes a disorganised tip as your once beautiful house disappears under this spreading babystuff. And you can soon begin to feel you are drowning under the labour of tidying.

To feel better about it you need is a perspective change.

However beautiful, organised, tidy and comparable to House Beautiful magazine your house was, now is not the time for it to be a major focus of yours.

For this period in time, it isn't really necessary to keep on top of it all. It doesn't matter. It isn't a valuable part of being a good mum and can wear you ragged continually trying to maintain it.

Now is the time to let it go and rethink your priorities.

Now is the time for a 'lived-in' look. Now is the time for a real lived-in *home* not a show house. You are home-making not show-making.

Now is the time for a *busy loving* home.

You have a busy, breathing, bouncing, loveable child. A child that is *much, much, much more precious* than a show house. A child that needs you to be involved in his busy, breathing, bouncing life. Not stressed out trying to keep his busy life tidy.

Tidy is *not* important for now. This time with your child *is*. It will soon be over. Don't miss it while you are busy worrying about your house being tidy.

It doesn't matter what friends and neighbours think. Or relations. It doesn't matter what anyone else thinks. What matters is that YOU are not stressed. There's nothing more stressful than trying to tidy busy lives away all the time. Don't worry about it. You are a mum now – a mum has other duties the most important of which is nurturing a child.

Apart from that your child needs stimulation. A tidy house is not nearly as stimulating to look at as one that's filled with interesting stuff. And *all stuff* is interesting to a small child however boring or untidy it seems to us.

Forget tidy – keep a little organised certainly as it makes life easier - but go for a lived-in stimulating look. Lived in homes are happy homes. I'd much rather be in a lived in home any day. The minute I walk into an immaculately tidy show house I feel dulled to boredom. A mum who is fussed about always being tidy doesn't make a happy mum.

If tidy is that important to you, try and change your thinking, rethink your perspective, compromise. Win some bits, lose others. It will make you happier to accept this is how it is for now rather than to trying to keep it how it was and fight to maintain something that is not as important as being a good parent. A good parent values their parenting over tidy. I'm not suggesting you live in a slum; you just have to get a workable perspective on it. A workable perspective also teaches your child about managing their stuff too, about having a workable perspective in their lives to come. That's what they need, not stress over tidy.

Changing your perspectives on other domestic jobs

That goes for other jobs in the home too. All jobs that have no impact on your child what so ever are jobs you might like to consider ditching for a while.

Jobs like cleaning windows. Always hoovering. Ironing babygrows – or ironing anything for that matter. Dusting. Constant cleaning and wiping.

If it doesn't have an immediate effect on the health and welfare of your child then forget it for a while. It doesn't matter. And with regard to health and welfare, despite what we're emotionally blackmailed to do through mass commercial advertising of cleaning and hygiene products, constantly wiping surfaces your child is going to touch with revolting chemicals is as harmful to the wider planet your child will inhabit as if you didn't. Clean water will do and it doesn't have to be constant. Don't be blackmailed by insidious marketing.

Aesthetically speaking, your child doesn't care whether the windows are clean or not, whether her babygrows are ironed or not, whether her bed is made or her toys put away. What she cares about is having an attentive and contented mum. Not one who's stressed about house perfect.

Smooth lives are far, far more important than smooth clothes.

A little story

The mums I know have a little message; don't waste your child's infancy on unimportant housework.

*Most of the mums I know altered much of what they considered important. Most of them now say that housework isn't important. The housework will still be there when your kids are gone. You can make up for it then. But you can **never** have this time to be with your tiny child again.*

I'm not suggesting abandoning all previous standards, all cleanliness and tidiness. But we can be obsessed with show and are certainly obsessed with sterile at the moment. And we're killing the planet meanwhile, but as long as big business empires rule then that seems to be a secondary consideration. Yet the ironic thing is that it is the legacy we leave our kids – a polluted planet. We need to think ecologically about our behaviours, our impact and what's important, both to our small child right now, and to the wider world. We really don't need to be as obsessively clean and bleached as advertising would condition us to believe. And our kids need exposure to a few germs to build up immunity.

Look at which jobs *really* are important. Find a balance between giving jobs your time and giving children your time. Don't become one of the women I've met who've missed out on the enjoyment of their child because they were busy coping with domestic trivia. Or perhaps hiding behind it!

Coping isn't about perfection. It's about finding a balance which suits you as a mum now. And before you worry in case you're 'dropping' your standards here's a thought to help: *Standards don't 'drop'. They change.*

Changing your perspectives on time

During my working life prior to having babies my life was run according to my watch. I think that's probably the same for anyone who's been employed outside the home.

Small children and babies don't read watches. They don't care what the time is. They only care about a few things; food, sleep, comfort and stimulation. Trying to schedule events according to the clock can be extremely frustrating.

Clocks make us time stressed. When actually *we don't need to time our job of being a mum.*

I'm not saying we never have times and schedules to keep. Of course we do. But what we don't have to do is to maintain a clock run day out of habit.

The coming of a baby drastically changes how your day is run. It seems to upset all your previous routines and its own personal routine takes over.

This doesn't matter. This does change. And it's a lot easier to go with it than to maintain unimportant schedules out of habit.

It actually doesn't matter *when* you get up in the morning, particularly if you've got the opportunity to catch up on sleep.

It doesn't matter really *when* you get dressed, *when* you get the washing on, *when* you get the pots washed, even *when* you go to bed. Go to bed at seven if you're tired.

Clock time is less important than taking time to do things in a way that you are comfortable with. If you are comfortable your child is comfortable. It makes things easier all round.

Feed your baby when you wish. Do what needs to be done when it suits you now not when it suited before out of habit. Take time out when it's offered no matter what time of day it is.

And the other change in your time perspective you might want to be aware of is to do with the habit of *rushing*.

Current working culture seems to applaud rushing. We all seem to be rushing. That's because we think we have to pack more in, to appear to be busy, busy, busy in order to feel important. We all seem to be scared we're going to run out of time. Or going to be less of a person if we pack less into a day.

The only time that you're going to run out of now is *time with your child*. And you're only going to be less of a person if you can't see why that matters.

It matters because it *takes time* to develop a child. Rushing upsets the child and stresses you out. It belittles this important job. Be aware if you are unnecessarily rushing. Take time to slow down. Slowing down relaxes you. Relaxing feels good. You're more of a person relaxing into your mumhood timing than sticking to one for old image's sake.

It is easy to become obsessed with this rushing working tempo. With multi-tasking, with pulling in as many jobs as you can all at the same time.

You don't need it now. Your tempo needs to be a relaxed tempo – not a rushed working one. Things still get done. I'm not talking about dossing around. I'm talking about a purposefully more relaxed way of working through the things that need to be done. Rushing doesn't always mean you are achieving things any quicker. It usually means you are achieving things stressfully. It doesn't have to be like that.

Be aware of time. Change your point of view.

Changing your perspective on the label 'work'

Most of us use our 'work' as a way of validating ourselves. Of making ourselves feel worthy. Whether that work is outside or inside the home.

Many women feel the need to be seen to be 'busy' in order to feel worthy. That's understandable because that is unfortunately how much of society judges people. By how 'busy' they are.

I believe mums have a different worth. I believe that mums' true worth is to do with bringing up their children and that requires time and attention to *love*. Not *busy*.

Now I don't want to give the wrong impression here. I don't want anyone to think I'm suggesting that mums are not busy. I've already said that mums are the hardest workers of all society.

But you have to remember not to work so hard that you *don't have time for love*. Or that you work so hard for the simple reason that work gives you something to show for what you've done all day and love doesn't.

Some mums find it hard to value what they do if what they do has nothing tangible to show for it.

Love is as important a part of your day's work as all the other jobs being a mum involves.

And you don't have to worry that you've got nothing to show for how hard you've worked at loving your child. Because *one day you will* have something to show. You will have a mature, well-adjusted, and happy child who has self-worth and the self-confidence to tackle anything. A mum more concerned with seeming to be busy than with love won't have that.

This love takes some time out of your day. Lots of time actually. That is as an important part of your work as any other 'busyness'. This counts as work too. And this loving part can make you feel fantastic.

It's the *real payoff*.

The love bit is more important than the labour – the jobs - everything.

Getting involved by giving your child attention produces the *most rewarding moments* in the whole of your mothering life. It makes you feel love and love makes you happy. Getting involved makes you happy. It builds this *wonderful loving relationship which lasts for life*. Investing time to it now gives you a lifetime's annuity. Don't miss paying into it for the sake of being 'busy' in the eyes of others as that's often what bugs us – appearing to be 'busy' in the eyes of others.

Your job of loving and paying attention to your child is the most valuable work you could be doing and will eventually make such a positive difference to the world because one day your child will spread that love around. Pay attention to it and you will be adding worth and showing worth to your child.

I want to talk about that worth and value a lot more later on in the book but for now:

- Give yourself credit for doing the job of loving your child.
- Credit yourself with your time it's taking.
- Feel the worth of it.

To recap:

<u>Thinking about your work as a mum</u>:

- Appreciate what a *big workload* you have and how hard you work to be a mum.
- Appreciate the difficult *conditions* you work under and go easy on yourself.
- Don't forget to concern yourself with the *loving* bits as well as the work, they are much more important.
- Allow your perspectives to *change* for this period in time, it's soon over.
- Re-assess your *priorities*.
- The working hours are demanding, remember to have *time off*.
- Where you haven't the support of family around you to help, don't be afraid to allow others to *support* you through this labour intensive time.
- *Credit* yourself with time out, time off, and time away from your child.
- Don't be a workaholic. Be a *love*aholic!
- Beware multi-tasking, rushing and 'being busy' and *slow down*.

- Look after yourself – you're a *champion* worker – you need to recharge.
- If you're becoming stressed choose to do it *differently*.
- *Enjoy your child* – don't let time with her pass you by.

Tip-Bit No 4: Nappies and Beyond

What's the big deal about nappies?

Looking back it's easy for me to say that isn't it? But when you've just got this delicate baby-bird thing with limbs home alone changing a nappy can seem as daunting as making a fifteen course meal for the in-laws.

Don't worry

Nappy changing is no big deal. You'll soon have it off to such a fine art you'll be able to do it with one hand whilst balancing the baby on your knee under the table at your favourite café, drinking a coffee with the other hand and still keeping a conversation going about pelvic floor exercises with your friends.

Believe me – it's true.

Experts, advertising, and the media would have us believe that a healthy baby's bum is impossible to achieve without this, that, or the other product, without a particular baby changing table at a particular height, without matching accessories and the inevitable changing bag. And if the baby's bum gets sore it's all your fault.

Well, you'll be pleased to hear that none of that is true.

All babies' bums need is a quick clean. At any height, even the bench in the precinct if it's all that's available, and a clean nappy. And babies' bums sometimes get sore at some point however careful you are. It's not necessarily your fault.

You *don't* need masses of cleaning products – gels, creams, talcs, scented wipes etc. - for your baby to be comfy even though the companies who make these products try their hardest to convince us otherwise. They don't give a toss about your baby's bum really, or the planet for that matter, so don't be conned by them.

You *can* totally suit yourself over which nappies to use; all have drawbacks, all have advantages, all have an ecological impact despite what the guilt trippers would have us believe.

Manufacturers do not know what's best for you and your baby – you do. You *don't* have to wake the baby to change it as specific times of the clock as some idiots suggest. It *is* easy with practise, not paraphernalia, and you get plenty of that.

The less paraphernalia you have the quicker it is. The quicker it is the better for baby. Better for mum. Better for all the other customers in the coffee shop who have to endure the smell.

No fuss. No bottles. You don't need cream every time if it's a fast change. Just a clean nappy. And a wipe. Or spit on a tissue if it's all you've got which is probably a better option than chemical products anyway.

Like this you can change a baby quickly and discreetly anywhere. In the park. Across your knee. Back of the car. On the bus. In the buggy.

Once you start fussing with all the other stuff commercial hype thrusts at us you take far too long and end up with a restless screaming baby. Or a toddler trying to wriggle away, or pee everywhere.

Obviously babies bums do need a good clean. Very regularly. Like a bath every night if they've been really dirty. But a ritual as precious as the Chinese Tea Ceremony is not essential every time. I know it's all lovely having this new immaculate stuff, but it soon changes its pristine appearance and just becomes a nightmare in fiddle once you've done it a few hundred times and have got umber smears in the cream.

So; just lay baby down, floor level is the safest (never turn away from a baby on a changing table – my friend did - it fell on the floor – don't worry, it was fine). Undo suit. Undo nappy. Reel from shock of contents. Quick wipe, often with a clean bit of old nappy, put new nappy under. Smear on cream. Do up nappy. Wipe pee off hand. Wriggle baby's legs back into suit. Keep it smooth, keep it calm and don't always rush, make the baby giggle; it works better that way.

Simple.

It's hell if they've got to the stage where they keep walking off. But perhaps then is the time to consider change.

Leaving nappies behind

Believe me; it's a lot simpler when they're still in nappies. Although it's not until you're standing well enmeshed in that hours long queue in the Post Office that they say "mum, I want a wee!" that you realise how simple.

Is that 'I *think* I want a wee', or 'I want a wee *desperately*'? You look at his face. It's concentrating. And knees are pressed together. Hands clutching crutch. You look round hopelessly for a loo.

Thus it gets to the time when they come out of nappies and begin to use the potty, loo, behind a tree, down the side of Boots, behind the car. You're into the realm of wee and whoopsie watching because that's a bit what it's like.

I'm not going to use the term Potty Training. I don't even believe in potty training. It suggests something far too regimental for my liking, like some sort of sadistic training some sergeant major puts you through and the way some mums behave you'd believe it was.

I've seen perfectly nice, sweet loving mums turn into the Gestapo under the guise of potty training.

I've seen kids' bare bums smacked for not getting the pee in the right place at the right time.

I've heard sergeant majors forcing their kids to sit on the toilet for hours until they've performed. And neurotic ones asking their kids if they want a wee every five seconds (I think I did that at first).

Then I've heard mums complaining about their children deliberately 'holding it', and other weird behaviours like pooing in desperation behind the settee – the child that is, not the mother.

Poor little kids. The only training that takes place in these circumstances is training them not to be comfortable with their functions, or not to function at all. Which is a horrendous state of affairs.

Weeing and pooing is *no big deal*. We all do it. Even the queen. We all get the hang of it eventually – there's *no time limit*. Keep that thought in mind and take away any pressure from your child. A bursting bladder is pressure enough. If your child seems wildly different to everyone else's or you're worried seek professional advice but don't be too influenced by everyone else's time frames. Your child is an individual.

I believe there are several things that have to happen before an infant becomes able to use the loo in the way we do.

a)   They have to see the way we use it and appreciate all folks do that, and why it's desirable.

b) They have to be aware of their own bodily functions and be comfortable with them.

So they have to have developed sufficiently physically and in maturity. Then they have to be able to control those bodily functions, even if only to a small degree at first. And until those conditions are reached then there's no point in 'training'.

But what you can do is start to bring these matters to the attention of your child. Like seeing you use the toilet – if your house is anything like ours nothing's private anyway. Like leaving the nappy off at times so it becomes noticeable what's happening. Like showing them where to sit if they want to. (Potty or loo, it's up to them). It will take lots of practise for your child to get used to what it feels like and maintain a comfortable relationship with their bodily functions and the results of them.

Never get into a state. (Difficult – I know – but do try).

Leading your child towards using the toilet can be a tense and agitated slog through a minefield. Or it can be hilariously funny. It's up to you.

The child's happiness with it all is essential. Your calmness with it all is essential. It really doesn't have to be the big deal some folks make of it. It is just as natural a part of your child's development as you encouraging them to walk – when they're ready – don't make any more of a deal of it than that.

Wee on the carpet is inevitable. Holding small children in cramped positions whilst your back's breaking and they're straining is also inevitable. As is standing in public toilets for ages reading the graffiti while they strain away. It's no big deal.

They're not going to get it right straight away. But they soon will. They are going to be frightened maybe at times. You need to be constantly reassuring and full of praise for that wonderful pile they've just dropped in the plant pot, but could you have it in the potty next time.

And you also need to be completely competition proof against anyone who suggests you *should* be training your child *by now*. The *when* is only up to you and your child.

If you've got a good relationship with your child, they'll want to please you. And they try so hard. Let it be them trying, not you. They'll do it themselves when they can. There are *bound* to be accidents. Don't make them an issue. They're quite funny really.

<u>A little story</u>

One of mine was determined. She wanted to get it right, but couldn't seem to settle on the toilet, partly because she was busy wearing the special seat round her neck, so I busied myself running the bath. As soon as my attention was diverted she did a heaper on the floor not being able to get on the toilet quick enough. So I scooped it up and put it in the potty, which was also available, to show her where it should be. Meanwhile she whipped my socks out of the laundry basket, wiped her bottom on them and then protested strongly for me to get the poo out of the potty so she could wear it on her head.

Next time she managed to get on the toilet and after heaving and straining and conversations through gritted teeth there's a plop. I say 'well done', she wants to wipe herself and accidentally flicks a sausage onto the floor. I take a step forward looking for it and put my foot in one she'd already done. I was wearing the same aforementioned socks.

After all that she's an expert now. It all comes with patience.

There's no time limit. There are no rules. There's no training required. No gadgets necessary. Don't buy new carpets until they're at least sixteen by which time it'll be drink that's spilled on them.

And like with everything else with children, the less fuss *you* make the better, and it's all over very, very *quickly*.

You mustn't laugh outright at them but don't forget to **smile**! It will make this sometimes frustrating and anxious time a whole lot *happier*!

Chapter Five

Role-overview

It matters that mums enjoy mumhood. It's one of the most important jobs in the world – so it's important to enjoy it because you'll make a better job of it.

Actually, I'd like all mothers to enjoy it and be happy. Because this mostly makes for happy children. That makes the relationships between parents and children happy ones too. Then that makes a happy community and happier world to live in.

It's a bit of a tall order but wouldn't it be great if it was like that?

Wouldn't it be great to see happy mums with great big happy smiles on their faces, enjoying pushing their toddlers round in the trolley as they talk through all the mundane stuff you gab on about with your child to keep them stimulated? It's an art talking about baked beans and making it seem interesting. I love seeing mums engaged in doing this as if it one of the most purposeful things they could be doing. Which it is and if you're one of those this chapter may not be relevant to you.

But I don't seem to see that much.

More often I see rushed and stressed, harassed and often cross mums with whinging children and obvious fatigue. Mums who fight not only to get the trolley to go in the right direction, but who also fight the mounting waves of frustration and resentment.

Now, I'm normal too - I feel frustration and irritation pushing a wayward trolley sideways just as much as the next mum. Particularly if I've got two restless children in tow. It does nothing for me.

But I don't think that's the biggest cause of the resentment and unhappiness I see in some mums. That I hear in their voices as they tell me the latest instalment of hardship of their lives. Or I sense in the heaviness and weariness of their body language or the weight in their faces.

I think it is all to do with something else. But that something else is not something that most mums are aware of.

Most mums think their feelings of stress, irritation, and discontent are to do with some of the mundane things about being a mum. Or by having an irritating little wind-up merchant round them all day. Or by being over tired, under-rested, sore, or hormonal.

And to an extent it is. Children can be as irritating as they are beautiful. And being with them all the time can be as exhausting as it is exciting. Adjusting to motherhood and the toll it takes is draining, and the millions of little jobs you have to do as a mum can easily make you feel discontent and dreary with the tedium of them. There is no doubt about that.

But there is something else too that contributes to these raging negative feelings that steal away the opportunity for mothers to be happy.

And that something is to do with role. It is to do with the role you adopt once you become a mother.

What does role mean?

Your role, in case you're not quite sure, is the part you play as the mother of your child, your function – as a *parent*.

Probably your role is never something you've had to think about or sort out in your life before. It's usually already mapped out for you.

When you started out as a child yourself, you probably didn't ever think about such complicated things. We don't seem to have much say as children anyway – we just got told. That's how it felt being a child.

Then you were a teenager whose role was to be stroppy or a student whose role was to appear to study but actually it was more importantly to have a good time. Or perhaps you went straight into work.

If you're lucky enough to be employed your role is clearly defined. You have a job description and your role comes out of that. It's mostly decided for you, duties are laid down and your job is to stick to it and fulfil a brief. And that role switches when you leave the place of employment for the day and take on a more recreational role of play.

But employed or not, usually whatever you're doing in life you've had a clear idea of what your role is, or what you want it to be, and how that's a priority.

Then maybe you moved in with a partner and your role shifted from being a single person to being part of a twosome but you're so besotted you don't notice anyway and life flows on and you don't really think about role at all because you're fairly happy with it.

But when you become a mother – BANG! All those roles that you played before are suddenly altered. They fade into insignificance. Everything changes. There's suddenly a whole new emphasis – a baby! And you're left high and dry on the shore with a completely new role; one of being a mum.

But actually – what is that, for goodness sake?

Generally, all through our life we never had to think about what our roles were. We kind of fell into them. Or our roles were mostly determined for us. And if we weren't happy with them we changed them. They were mostly clear cut. Often actually written down. Immediately recognisable – although we probably never needed to actually recognise or think about them really.

Until now.

So, isn't the role of a mother clear-cut and clearly defined?

No, it isn't. Because it's *personal and individual*. Because it's flexible. Because it's constantly changing. Because it incorporates so many *differing roles*. And because you really do have some *choice* in shaping it.

And if you want to enjoy being a mum then *you* need to think carefully about what you want *your role to be now*, what you want to do as a mother, and to *decide for yourself*.

Now you may be thinking that your role is already determined for you by the fact that you have a child. And to a great degree it is.

You are a mother. You have a child. Your *primary* role is to care for it. That's true.

But the *way* in which you do that brings many, many other roles into play that need specifically clarifying. For example; your primary role now is not only to push and fill that wayward trolley, but to *take more time over it so you can give the child sitting in it your attention too*. The focus of everything you do has changed. But you'll need to change the way you think to accommodate it. That is; if you're going to enjoy being a mother from now on in and not get bogged down trying to fulfil too many briefs.

Thinking about role:

To understand your role as a mum you need to think about and clarify;

- Your role with your child
- Your role in the home
- Your role with your partner
- Your role in the wider family
- Your role and work outside the home

Your role with your child

So what is your role as a mum?

Obviously your primary role with your child is to care for it. To look after it. To see to its health and wellbeing and safety.

But the trouble is some mums, as they look after their child, get tied up in knots whilst distinguishing what that *looking after* entails.

They think that looking after means always having dazzling white babygrows. Or a certain style of buggy to take the baby out in. Or the 'right' nappies. Or sticking to one particular style of parenting. Or giving the child what it wants and never saying no. Or earning lots of money so that the child can have the 'best' things in life and be seen in the 'right' designer wear. Or looking after everyone else too. Or always coping. Or maintaining an image of a perfect mother.

Now I don't see a mother's role like that at all.

I see my role as a mother looking after my children as one that concerns my time spent *with* my child – my interaction with them. I see my role is to nurture and comfort. Stimulate and educate (yes – even when they're tiny by talking to them about stuff) and encourage. To protect and keep safe. To support, guide and develop. And most of all to LOVE and love does sometimes mean saying 'no', even being separate sometimes when it's in the wider interest to do so.

And to do that I need to be spending my time giving my *child* attention, rather than spending my time giving all that other stuff attention.

This is the part of my role that I think is the most important. This is the part of my role that is most important to the child. The part that helps a child to develop. The part that makes them feel safe and loved. That gives them a happy childhood. That helps create another valuable member of society.

Through the times when their parent has been there. With them.

Your child is not going to remember you as the 'best mother in the world' because you ironed her babygrows, or bought her the right stuff. She's going to remember you as the 'best mother in the world' because you always *had time for her*.

Your role of caring for your child is not so much about what you do *for* your child as what you do *with* them.

And not only that, what you do *with* them is the bit that gives you the most happiness because that's the bit that builds that wonderful relationship.

And the relationship is where the pleasure and joy comes from.

To be there to witness those first smiles, first steps, first words – so many firsts. They are the rewards for being a mother. *And* all the other bits ever after - even the less significant bits, which are just as wonderful.

Those snugly times when you both drop off to sleep together one afternoon. Or share a special book. Or greet your child in the morning. Or are there to meet them when they come home. Or tuck them in last thing at night. Or stroke their flushed cheeks and damp curls after a bath. Gems and ingots of motherhood indeed.

Of course there are loads of things that you need to do *for* your child. We talked about that workload in the last section. But what I'm suggesting is that you keep them in proportion with the more important and rewarding role of interacting *with* them and giving your child your time and attention.

Your time and attention is a large important part of your role as a mother and parent. Some parents worry that too much attention will spoil a child and make them 'attention seeking'. Children are only attention seeking when they *don't* get it. You do have to balance giving them attention with giving yourself the necessary space too – I'm not saying smother! I'm just saying that it takes time and attention to be involved and interact.

Being involved is the bit that holds the key to so much pleasure. Just spend time enjoying your child as she grows. You will *never* have this role to play with this child again. It will change constantly. It will *never remain the same*. Enjoy everything you can about it.

Enjoy relaxing with them, playing with them, holding and rocking and nursing them. Laughing and giggling with them. Talking to them. Showing them the birds and the flowers and the trees and the buildings and the cars and the people and the wonderful world. Telling them stories. It all means so much to them. It's the best role you could ever be playing.(More to help with this in chapter 8; Mother and Child).

Don't worry if her-next-door has a tidy house. Don't worry if that mum at the toddler group gets more done than you. Don't worry if your friend always finds time to make things for the charity stall. Their kids won't be getting their mother's attention in the same way as yours is. YOU decide what's a more important role for YOU to play in your child's life. One based on what YOU think is right not what others are doing. YOU DECIDE. Find a balance that works for you.

Being true to what YOU decide is what gives you a greater chance of being happy with your role as a mother. Copying the role pattern of others will not. And that goes for your role within the home too.

Your role in the home

Being happy with your role in the home can be tricky.

Most particularly tricky for those who don't take easily to domesticity. Like me. Because it is the domestic bit that makes it tricky; the bit about who does what with all the cleaning up, washing up, mopping up, meal getting and tidying up which seems to increase tenfold when a baby appears.

If there's one role that I see makes many women unhappy and resentful it's this one. It's to do with the fact that despite being able to contemporise their roles in the workplace, women still have not been able to contemporise their role within the home particularly when they become mums. And despite many wonderful modern day fathers and partners, there are still plenty of them about who are quite content to dump the domestic role on any woman who's willing to take it.

House*work* aside, it takes time and management to create a *home*. It doesn't just happen itself. And *home* making and all the *management* it requires usually always gets left to mums.

<u>A little story</u>

I have a mum friend who made a statement very early on in her motherhood that puts it very succinctly. She made a very important distinction for all of us – one that you may have been completely unaware of. One that made her hugely unpopular with the in-laws. But for which I have huge respect.

She said 'I may have been willing and happy to take on the role of mother. But I'm not willing or happy to take on the role of housewife' (meaning; do all the housework).

Love it! I love it because she makes the correct *distinction* between the two.

Because they *are* separate. And should be treated separately. And I believe it is the fact that these roles are not treated separately, are not discussed separately (or at all for that matter), which can make many mums unhappy and even resentful. And sometimes that resentment overflows onto the children.

Tradition is to blame. Good old tradition sticking housework on women like chewing gum sticks to your shoe and about as welcome. This is what makes many women miserable – having to fulfil this cloying role of doing all the domestic stuff – when most of them just don't want it – when it may have been shared before.

The other trouble is we're good at it. Men usually aren't – or choose not to be! So we often take it on or get landed with it.

And it particularly happens when you are a mother at home full-time and you are *unaware* that you can make the distinction. When you are unaware that just because you are a mother doesn't mean you have to suddenly do all the cleaning too. When you and your partner don't talk about it. When you find yourself smothered by traditional thinking even in today's so-called emancipated world.

I said right at the start that this book was about thinking differently. That to be happy with being a mum you would perhaps have to think differently about a few things.

Thinking differently from the traditional view of the role of mother, as in housewife who suddenly becomes the person who does all the stuff required to run a home, is perhaps one area where you have to do that most of all. Not only that – you might have to change a few other minds as well.

This is how I think about it: I see that *two* partners (or husband and wife although 'partners' better describes the relationship without a sense of possession) who are parents, have *three* jobs between the *two* of them. (If there's only one of you and you're a single mum you are the greatest champion of all – you have my deepest respect).

The three jobs are; a) the wage earning b) the parenting and c) the domestic stuff. And in a world of equality they should be *equally shared* or resolved to the satisfaction of *everybody*. Each job should be individually discussed between partners, with each partner having a satisfying amount of opportunity to play the role they want. Whether it is parenting, work outside the home, or the housework.

It's worth thinking about. It is worth sorting out. To make *both* of you, mum and dad, happy with the role you now play as parents. And to make quite sure you, as a mum, are happy with the role you end up with.

It is important to remember that the role of mother does not necessarily have to come with the role of 'person who does all the housework' already attached. You need to make the DISTINCTION. You need to DECIDE whether to do all the domestic work is a role you want. You need also to remember that just because you are at home all day with your child it doesn't necessarily mean that you have to do all the mucking out – including mucking out for everyone else particularly those who can do it for themselves.

That DOES NOT have to be part of your role as a mother. Agreed; it is something that needs doing – but how and when and by whom needs *democratically deciding* between you *both*. And I'm hoping you have a partner who supports you in this.

Giving up full-time, paid, stimulating work outside the home to play the valuable role of parent is one thing. Giving up stimulating work to be a cleaner or servant or skivvy is another. Fine if you want it. Needs sorting if you don't. Don't let traditional thinking obscure individual thinking. It's up to YOU.

I appreciate that there are many single mums for whom this is not a choice as you have no one with whom to share this workload. For you I think it's even more important to carefully prioritise what jobs really need doing and what can be left as I talked about in the previous chapter. And to accept any offers of help to deal with it. And skip the next section!

Your role and your partner

Once you and your partner become parents both of your roles immediately change. Of course they do – you're parents now. But what also changes is the dynamics between you – and that does make a difference. Your relationship will have to weather this turbulent sea of change for a while. You both have some adjustments to make. You have lots of talking to do. You will both need to sort out your roles now.

If you are a mum at home now, when you weren't before having a child, you will be the one having the most dramatic change in your daily life.

Being at home with your child, having the opportunity to love it and care for it and watch it develop, is wonderful.

Caring for your children is the best thing you could be doing. As important a role as any other in family life.

But caring for your children does not extend to caring for your partner as if he were a child too. This is another traditional pitfall that I see mums fall into.

Just as women no longer have to be financially 'kept', men don't have to be 'looked after' in the traditional sense of the word. Tradition again to blame for sticking an unnecessary workload on women at home.

Reciprocal caring is part of any relationship. Each helping and supporting where it is needed – that's what a loving relationship is. But what I see happening to some mums is often not reciprocal. It is often one-sided.

It is often the women going into caring overdrive and awarding the same level of looking after to their partners, as they do to their children, as if their partners were children too. And their partners are not going to turn it down and what started out as occasional becomes a habit, becomes expected, and before you know where you are you're on overload. It just so easily happens.

It happens for all sorts of reasons.

It happens because it was traditional for women to look after their men. It happens because it was the traditional role of a woman at home. It happens because women at home full-time are trying to seek some kind of approval both from their partners and from their families. It happens because some women are naturally caring. It happens because women are natural givers and they give of themselves in this way. It happens because many women put others before themselves. It happens because some men think it's their right to be looked after in this way since they work outside the home and in their view this is more valuable than the work mums do. It happens as a way for some women to justify their existence when they don't earn any money. (That's a big issue!) It happens because some partners expect it. It happens because some partners abuse the vulnerable position a woman is sometimes in...

It happens for so many reasons. But when it happens without you *choosing* it you can soon become resentful of it.

Mothers often fall into pitfalls. Mopping up after someone who is able to do it for themselves just because you happen to be at home is a pitfall many fall into. It is what I hear mums grieving over as much as anything to do with mothering their *child*.

You and your partner will need to constantly *discuss and review* each of the roles that you now need to take on. *Continually*. Because they will *continually* change.

That's what parenting is like – like the British weather – *changeable*! Talk about it as you ride it out. Be aware. Exercise choice.

Your role and your wider family

What also will have changed is your role within the eyes of others.

Now what has that got to do with anything?

It shouldn't really have anything to do with the role you decide to take on – as it's up to you – we've already said that. But often what happens is that the opinions and expectations of others can seriously affect what you do as a mother. It can seriously undermine your decisions to play it how you want. To *do what you want*.

The thinking you are doing now about being a mum is brilliant. It is what's going to make you handle it well and consequently be a happier mum. Decisions about your role as a mum are going to be the results of that thinking.

But not everyone is going to think about it in the way you do. That *doesn't* make you *wrong*. Yet it might perhaps make you *different* in the eyes of all those traditional thinkers who have fallen into traditional roles. And I wouldn't be surprised if within your family you come across quite a few traditional thinkers.

It is quite hard to stick out for the things *you* want against ingrained traditional thinkers, especially family members.

But it is important you do what you want with your role as a mum. That's what will make you a happy mum. Not doing what everyone else expects.

I want to talk about 'Expectations' and handling the influence they have on you in more depth in the next chapter. But I wanted to bring it up here, as you are thinking about your role, because it will make a difference and I wanted to prepare you for that.

Listen to your family – they can be a great support and comfort. Look at their perspectives. But listen to YOUR gut feelings too. Keep a balance. Stand by your own original ideas. Have plenty of interaction with friends who support *you* in the role *you* want to play. This will give you strength to stick out for what you think is important.

Stick out for happiness and wellbeing of your new little family rather than, or as well as, tradition. *Choose what works for you.*

It is *your* right to do so.

Your role and work outside the home

Just as it is your right to choose your role within your home, it is equally your right to choose your role outside of it.

I believe *parenting is a full-time job*. I believe that to do that job well your family now needs full attention. But I don't necessarily believe that it is the role of the woman to do it all the time.

Some women feel that their work as a mum requires them to be full-time with their child and they'd like to. Some women feel that to be a good mum to their child they need to have other stimuli outside the home too.

Being at home full-time with pre-school children is not a job every woman wants. Just as it is not a job every man would want. That needs discussing. It should not be automatically assumed that a man has first choice about the work outside the home.

Each of you, both the mum and dad, has to find a balance between the work that requires doing now you are parents and the role you want to play in the home and out of it.

You will need to discuss the balance of roles of *both parents* between you. You will perhaps need to rethink the traditional view that it is the mother at home with the child *all* the time. You will perhaps have to resist the influences of other traditional thinkers. You may want to make the decision to be there for your child full-time *despite* the fact that it was not your original intention. You may want to play a traditional role because it works for your circumstances. You may not. You may want full time work outside the home. You and your partner might want to *share* in the job of bringing in an income and *share* in the job of parenting, which might require your partner to work *less*. That *is* another way of doing it, often overlooked. Another option - your partner might want to do the full-time parenting.

These decisions can only be personal to you and your partner. But they *do need to be decisions*. Not roles you have just dropped into and you have become stuck with.

Feeling stuck in a role you didn't want is not going to help you enjoy your mumhood. And that's important for your children and your family life and to fulfil this valuable role of mum you now play.

And whatever role you choose remember it is likely to *change*. You *never* have to stay stuck. You *always* need to keep talking, choosing and deciding.

To recap on thinking about your role:

- Recognise the distinction between parent and housewife. Parenting and housework.
- Decide who does what on the housework front.

- Remember that being at home does not qualify you for all the domestic work too.
- Be aware of slipping into traditional roles you may not want.
- Be aware of the traditional pitfalls of being at home.
- Discuss roles with your partner.
- Discuss your relationship – important now you are parents.
- Beware caring over drive.
- Choose your roles both in and out of the home.
- Decide what's right for you.
- Be flexible.
- Keep reviewing – everything always changes.

Whatever you do – don't worry!

This might all seem a bit daunting – I understand that. After all, you've got enough to worry about with looking after a child now. Children are enough of a worry on their own without all these big concerns about role. Having a child brings enough daily decisions – some of them may be quite trivial but clubbed together they can form a mountain. You hardly need more decisions to make about your role and it may all feel right anyway.

So no need to worry, because if you're doing the right thing for you it will just *feel* right. Or, perhaps more noticeably; doing the wrong thing will *feel wrong*.

That's why I wanted to bring the above issues to your attention for you to keep in the back of your mind to think about only if you need to. They are *merely suggestions*.

Many mums do not have to think about any of this stuff at all. Many mums are perfectly happy the way they are.

But if things feel wrong it might help to think about some of the issues I've raised here. That's all. Otherwise don't sweat it. As they say; 'if it ain't broke don't fix it'!

Worrying about being a good mum brings with it all kinds of hang-ups. And one of the biggest hang-ups of all is living up to others' *expectations*.

Expectations can create a big barrier between you and feeling right about what you're doing. That's what I want to talk about next.

Meanwhile don't worry about being a good mum. As I said; a *thinking, caring mum is a good mum.*

You're obviously a good mum or you wouldn't be looking at this right now. You wouldn't be thinking about your motherhood in the way that you are.

There's only one thing better than being the good mum that you are. That is being a good mum *and* a happy mum. That's what we're working towards.

Tip-Bit No 5: Tantrums

Here's something that myself and other mums who have lived through it know to be true:

Tantrums are best ignored

Here's something else myself and other mums also know to be true:

Ignoring tantrums is almost humanly impossible!

But there's no doubt about it; any tantrum a child is throwing is almost always made **a whole lot worse** by you trying to do something about it.

Yet we've all gone blundering on either trying to pacify, or trying to make the child 'stop being silly', or just getting so wound up and cross we throw a tantrum ourselves. All perfectly understandable knowing the pressure and stress all mums work under all the time, especially in public.

None of it works though, does it?

Your child is usually far too upset to be pacified and anyway you can't make yourself heard over the roaring.

When your child is at boiling point she is not receptive to any kind of reasoning. To her, the way she's feeling is not 'silly' so you suggesting it just aggravates her. And since she's so devastatingly upset, you getting into a state too just frightens and inflames her further.

Shouting and smacking is definitely out. No. Far better to leave alone.

But how?

We all know a tantrum is the most upsetting experience for everyone. How can we ignore the feelings it evokes? Even more so in public, where there is particular pressure on mum to 'do something'.

Let's have a look at those feelings. Let's have a look at the way tantrums make mums feel. Because if we can deal with that, we are in a better position to cope with ignoring these terrible outbursts.

What makes mums upset with tantrums?

Obviously seeing and hearing someone in convulsions of rage and frustration does nothing to make us happy. But that aside, I guess the two fundamental reasons we get upset are:

a) We hate it when our child is so cross and upset and closed to reason especially when we can't do anything about it, and

b) We panic because we can't stop it, we're embarrassed about what others will think and that we've lost our control.

Actually these two reasons are almost inseparable. But let's start at a) the upset bit. Tantrums definitely are unbearably upsetting. **For the child and the mum.**

But ask; what is your child getting upset about in the first place?

Answer; probably through frustration and anger because they can't have what they want, or do what they want, or from awful pressure put upon them, in a situation they are not comfortable with, that they can't cope with, feelings they can't cope with.

Whatever reason, from the child's point of view it is *legitimate* that they are upset and it helps if you understand that. Making something out to be unimportant is devaluing your child's feelings. It *is* important from *their* point of view. We need to have sympathy for that fact.

But you don't have to get upset because they're upset. You don't have to be manipulated by them. You don't have to 'give in'. And you don't have to be *worried* by them being upset.

Your child *is* going to get upset at times and that is not always a bad thing. Love gets upset sometimes. It's inevitable. Your child will get over it, usually very quickly. The less fuss you make the quicker the process. You'll get over it too, although it takes longer. But we all survive.

You also need to understand that their tantrum is a *public* demonstration of their feelings and if you take away the audience they have no one to demonstrate their feelings to.

If you are in a situation where you can walk away from them, into another room, or the garden, or whatever, then it might help to do so. It also alleviates some of the tension that inflames these situations.

If you are in the supermarket checkout then it's not so easy. Very difficult to ignore when everyone's looking at you. When you feel sure everyone is thinking you're a terrible mum because you can't control your kid.

What you need to do is to know your child well enough to understand what it is that sparks off particular tantrums and upsets and try and avoid it. Think ahead.

Is there something you could really manage differently and so avoid causing all this distress? Is there a situation coming up where you think a tantrum might be inevitable, but which you could talk to your child about first to help them cope with it?

I'm not suggesting you give in to demands, but I'm never against a little compromise or negotiation or deviation from the original plan if it's going to make life easier and make mums and children happier. We're all happier without upset – that's what we're aiming for.

Tantrums in supermarket checkouts are often the result of the child not being bought the sweets the managers of supermarkets put at the checkouts exactly so children will manipulate their parents into buying them. Perhaps talking to your child, if they're old enough, about not making a fuss about sweets whilst you're out and they'll get a special reward for this behaviour when they get home, might help. Or distraction with toy from your ever-bulging bag might work for younger kids. Something to alleviate their boredom and restlessness.

Let's face it, going round supermarkets or shopping in general, as an example, can be an extremely boring and frustrating experience. So change the experience. Slow down and make the agenda not only getting the shopping but also getting your child's attention away from the boredom and restlessness by keeping them interested. Talk to them. Explain. Show. Pre-empt the boredom or frustration in as many of the things you have to do with your child as you can by engaging them or making the experience different. Think ahead.

Tantrums at home from frustration over not being able to do things are easier to ignore because generally no one else is looking. When it's just you and your child things are a lot easier to handle, aren't they? And no one else can hear the noise. So walk away even though they're upset.

As we've said, **ignoring tantrums is best.**

But something else that perhaps needs saying, something that you could repeat to yourself while your child is screaming his head off in the toyshop is

Ignoring your child's tantrum does not mean you're failing as a mum

This is where the trouble is. This is when mums panic. This is (b).

Mums seem to think that they have to be seen to be in control of their child's behaviour. But I look at it differently.

Being a good mum does not mean you have to be in control of your child's behaviour all of the time. You are in control of caring *for* them. Obviously you need to show them the way to care and be considerate. But some of their behaviour comes from *within them* and is not within your control and this is how it will be, and should be.

They are still developing, and learning to cope. They are still making mistakes. You cannot always help, or predict, how they will behave, predict their mistakes. You're not psychic – well, not to that degree anyway – I think we do as mums have some psychic powers. And neither do you want to be a control freak. The child has to take some responsibility for their behaviour.

Their tantrum is their *responsibility*.

It's **their** tantrum. Not yours. You can't help it – you're not failing as a mum because your child is having a tantrum. And your job is to guide your child towards having control over his own tantrum, learn how to manage his feelings as I've talked about you managing yours. Even better if you can manage to avoid outbursts, distract them from the upset so they learn how to distract themselves eventually.

At home, or when you're out, you still don't have to *do* anything. You're not failing in your responsibility as a mum by doing nothing.

Your responsibility comes when you have to pick up the pieces afterwards.

After a tantrum rage, after the reasons for the tantrum have changed from the original frustration to simply the *upset*, then is the time to get involved. I believe, by then, children are genuinely upset, often by the intensity of their feelings. You know what it's like when you get crying and you can't stop? They get themselves in that state too. So a good cuddle all round does everybody good.

I don't think we have to be frightened that we're rewarding the tantrum. We're not. We're offering comfort for the upset that's left behind.

You *don't* have to try and establish control over your child's feelings. Just try and control your own feelings, calm yourself down, until the trauma passes then be nice to you both. Try and avoid what caused it happening again.

Tantrums really wind *you* up. Have a strategy for coping with that and you'll have got them beat.

I believe the *less* we do and worry about tantrums the *quicker* they dissolve. And if your child gets absolutely no attention or payback what so ever for this kind of behaviour then I think they soon forget it (and adopt another ploy).

I tried to avoid situations that I think may cause a tantrum because it is just so upsetting. I don't consider this a cop out of having my own way, or giving in, I just think it's a wise way of nurturing my child, his feelings and our relationships by deviating from warfare and adopting a different route or strategy or tactic. I see no point in head on confrontation. We're the ones with the skill to avoid it, not the child. They'll learn from us.

But we are only human. We can't always work it out. Or predict it. Or control it. But if we can cope with ignoring it, we may have less to deal with in the future.

If yours are going through a tantrum throwing stage at the moment, be nice to yourself and take heart in the knowledge that, like all stages, **this stage will pass**, and there will be lots of other mums who understand and have sympathy for what you're going through. Probably even those in the supermarket. Many of them will have been through it. They're probably on your side.

And anyway, we can forgive this small being giving vent to his feelings of frustrations and rage. He can't help it. After all, plenty of adult beings do just the same thing in all sorts of bizarre ways and we forgive them, don't we?

Chapter Six

Great Expectations

Is being a mother what you expected? Is it turning out how you thought?

Are you doing what you thought you'd do, being what you thought you'd be, feeling what you thought you'd feel?

I have a suspicion that the truthful answer might be; 'well actually – no!'

There's just no imagining what it's really going to be like being a mother further on, is there; when you're on that exciting conveyor moving towards the birth? When you're expecting in more ways than one.

What did you expect – if at all?

I would imagine that perhaps you:

- Expected it to be easier, a doddle even.
- Expected life to be very much the same, except with a baby.
- Expected to have the same amount of time as before.
- Expected to feel the same as before.
- Expected your baby to lie peacefully in its cot or your child to play peacefully while you got on.
- Expected to be the same person as before except with a baby.

Or perhaps you didn't expect anything at that stage, but what you've got now you *didn't* expect.

I would guess you didn't expect:

- To be feeling the way you do.
- To be working so hard at work you never knew existed.
- To be feeling the way you do about your work inside and outside the home.
- To be feeling the way you do about your child.
- To see your former life disappear so rapidly.
- Your life to be like it is now.
- Motherhood to be like this.

All of you reading this book will have different expectations. Except for one. I think I might be right in guessing that there is one similarity between all mums; whatever your expectations were – you're now doing something different. And harder.

I would guess that the feelings you had when you were expecting, and the feelings you have when you've been a mother for a while, are probably *miles* apart. For, as I've said, *nothing* is as you expect with being a mother.

And that can sometimes mean big trouble!

Matching your expectations to reality

Psychologists tell us that in order to be happy our expectations about what is going to happen need to match what *actually is* happening, in reality.

Yet with motherhood that hardly ever seems to be the case.

So, are you doomed to unhappiness as a mother then?

No. Of course not. There's always something you can do about it. And what you need to do right now is look carefully at what you expected to happen and how those expectations have affected you in line with the reality of what *is really* happening.

The other big snag is – it isn't only your *own* expectations that have an effect on you. It is everyone else's too. It's your partner's, your family's, your peer groups', society's, the media's, and of course tradition. Not to mention other expectations related to your child and its development and behaviour.

These expectations you have, and those coming from around you, all infiltrate your awareness and have an effect on the way you feel. They will have affected your behaviour and your perceptions in ways you probably never realised. And not having realised you cannot protect yourself from the discontent that may be the result.

For example, being happy with what you do is going to be difficult if it is not something you necessarily have *chosen* to do but are doing just because you *expected* to be doing it. Like, perhaps, returning to work.

Did you expect to before you became a mum or did everyone around you expect you to? Or vice-versa; did you expect to be at home full-time and enjoy it? Are your feelings about these decisions different from what you expected? Do you feel differently now you actually are a mum?

Thinking about expectations:

Start by asking yourself: are you now doing;

- what you *chose* to do...or...

- what you *expected*?

- And do you want to *choose differently* now?

Once you become a mum your feelings can *change*.

You need to *change your expectations and possibly choices* along with them in order to remain happy with what you are doing.

The 'Should' Brigade

Living up to the expectations of others, however big or small those expectations are, is probably the biggest cause of misery to mothers. Living up to the expectations of others is like being at the mercy of what I call the 'Should' Brigade.

The 'Should' Brigade are that group of expectations/people/images/media/influences/traditions that suggest that you 'should' be doing this, or you 'should' be doing that, and it's these 'shoulds' that can cause you more angst than anything.

Let me show you what I mean. Below is a list of 'shoulds'. Some of them will be 'shoulds' you put on yourself. Some of them will have come from elsewhere.

'Shoulds' you might put upon yourself: - I 'should' be healed in two weeks - I 'should' be back at work after a few weeks - I 'should' be able to get on as I did before - I 'should' be back to my normal size after the birth - I 'should' enjoy being a mum - I 'should' want to go back to work - I 'should' want to be with my child - I 'should' be able to cope all the time.

Some 'shoulds' from others might be: - She 'should' put the baby down more - She 'should' give up work and be a proper mother - She 'should' get back to work - She 'should' make the child sleep in its own bed - She 'should' be able to make a proper meal - She 'should' keep the place tidy

- She 'should' be coping better - She 'should' stop giving the child so much attention.

These 'shoulds' are all *expectations*.

All sentences with 'should' in them are expectations. All these 'shoulds' conspire against you to make you feel bad. All these 'shoulds' and all 'shoulds' like them can *take away your choice*.

I believe that in order for you to enjoy your time with your child, your time of being a mother, the only 'should' you should be doing is *what is right for you and your child NOT what everyone else thinks you should be doing*.

As far as I see it: ALL 'SHOULDS' NEED BANISHING FROM YOUR THINKING. Even - and perhaps most especially – your own.

'Should' sentences can create non-flexibility. *Flexibility, adaptability, changeability, and choice* are what are required for you to *enjoy* your motherhood and are all actually necessary for you to do it well. 'Shoulds' restrict all those things. They most particularly restrict individual choice.

You are allowed to make *individual* choices about what you want and need to do. You know what's best for you and for your child. You will come to know this perhaps in consultation with others. But be guarded against letting that consultation become a 'should'.

Be aware of 'should' ideals and be strong in not allowing them to dictate to you how you want to be a mum to your child. Notice if your own expectations and those of others are putting pressure upon you in the form of a 'should'.

Banish the word 'should' from your conversation and self-talk. That's important for your personal happiness and for the role you play as parent. If you want you can replace it with 'could'. 'Could' leaves room for choice. 'Should' doesn't. Put 'could' in your thinking instead.

Expectations from advice

Expectations don't only come in the form of 'shoulds'. They come hidden in advice too.

You will probably be reading about looking after babies and children and parenting in general on websites and blogs, in baby books and magazines. There are loads of good ones to support you. And you will find all kinds of valuable advice.

Advice is valuable – it's valuable for supporting you through the minefield of decisions and skills and anxieties that descend upon you when you are a mum. And that's how it is intended; to support.

What happens sometimes though is that some women can read all about this 'ideal' way of being a mum – for any literature is going to give you the ideal – and turn it into an *expectation* of what they *should* be doing. And then make judgements about themselves in comparison to this ideal.

Just when you're all raw and emotional and worried anyway, which is why you turned to the advice in the first place, you may feel that you don't reach the ideal portrayed and you're left reeling because you're not achieving what you 'should' be achieving as a mum, according to the advice.

None of this is helpful or what advice is about.

That's why it's important to keep advice within the context it is intended; as support. NOT an *expectation* that you need to live up to.

With motherhood there is *seldom one* simple answer or *one* simple way of being a good mum. Expecting the advice you come across in magazines, books or on the Net to work for you as a simple answer to your problem is *not* realistic.

If the advice does not work for you it is NOT because you are doing it *wrong* and you are a bad mother. It's simply because *you are different*.

Being the good mother you are, you will be seeking advice. But you will need a wide cross section of advice; then you will need to sift through it and decide what's best for you.

But don't turn advice into an expectation or a 'should'. Keep it in perspective to what *you* think too.

And never look at it as a *judgement* about what you are doing.

Websites, Forums, baby books, magazines, etc., are often full of the perfect mother, the perfect baby, the perfect child, and the perfect relationship between the two. This is how advice sometimes comes across. And nothing makes you feel worse than expecting what you're doing to be as perfect as these glossy images and of course the media loves to promote glossy – it sells stuff! We must try to keep it in perspective.

<u>A little story</u>

I was never that perfect. My friends weren't. And thankfully my friends and I soon realised that reading all this stuff was all very well, but it could very soon make you feel you weren't making the grade as a mother as some of us began to feel. Luckily we had each other to keep a balanced perspective on it all.

No one is as perfect as ideals suggest. No one could be. They are just ideals, nice to look at but no one could expect to live up to that kind of perfect. And they are certainly not useful as expectations. Just as no one could expect to live up to the perfect image of an airbrushed photograph, perfect images of motherhood in the media can be just as airbrushed. Don't be fooled by them.

Ideals do have a place – it's nice to have ideals. They help us grow. But they're not necessarily what *you should* be doing. Keep realistic. Keep a perspective on where you're at. And keep happy rather than ideal. Never judge yourself in comparison to these ideals. Be confident in yourself and what you are doing.

You're better working towards a fulfilled and valued motherhood – not perfection. Mums and babies aren't perfect they're human and glorious as such. Don't expect them to be anything else. And don't be caught out by them – keep thinking.

<u>Thinking about things that might be expected but about which you have choice:</u>

- You don't *have* to use disposable nappies - Or - you don't *have* to use terry nappies.
- You don't *have* to get dressed by ten in the morning. You don't *have* to have your baby or child dressed by ten in the morning. Or at all!
- You don't *have* to go to the clinic. You don't *have* to go to toddler group.
- You don't *have* to always hold back the tears.
- You don't *have* to always cope or be organised.
- You don't *have* to be with your child all the time.

- You don't *have* to be at home full-time. You don't *have* to work full-time.
- You don't *have* to do what others are doing, what's suggested in the media, or what your mother or your in-laws say.
- You don't *have* to have lots of money or take the kids to Disneyland to be a good mum.
- You don't *have* to love every minute of being a mother.
- You don't *have* to be ashamed, feel guilty, feel bad about doing what *you* want.
- You don't *have* to be perfect.

Expectations on forums

Online forums provide a massive supportive network. It's so comforting to be connected to a network of caring supportive people who are going through the same things as you. And one day you'll be able to support others in the same way. Now we have forums no one needs to mother alone.

But they can also inadvertently be a massive drain on your confidence, not to mention another way for the 'Should' Brigade, or expectations, to overcome you if you're among mums who seem to have it all in control and forget the agenda is to support one another, not boast about what they're doing or judge one another. As much as being supportive, forums can also make you feel not as able as everyone else on there, so you have to be wise how you use them.

Writing on the web is tricky. Just like with texting we can give an impression that is not what we intended. Also some people use it as a place to spout off unpleasantly behind the shield of anonymity. And many are not so skilled at expressing what they want to express whilst writing anyway.

Remember this as you dip into forums and connect.

You can use forums for support and connecting with other mums. Equally you can move away from them if you don't feel supported. You have the *choice* to use them as and when you want.

Never allow anything on a forum to trample on your sensitivities. Manage how you use them – and how they're using you. Decide and choose which and where you read and contribute. Don't let forums become another barrage of expectation. And don't let forums replace the essential support of meeting up and connecting with real live mums as well.

Feeling sensitive to judgements of others

Becoming a mother is a very vulnerable time. Any time of change is. We sometimes don't expect that. You'll maybe feel very raw. You're healing. You're tired. You're worried about being a good mother. You're sensitive.

That is all very normal in a mum. Everyone I've talked to has felt like that. In particular they've felt very sensitive to the judgements of others.

It's bizarre but motherhood is one of those jobs everyone seems to think they're qualified to make judgements about. Everyone seems to think they know best – even those that have never done it. Or perhaps even more so the ones who haven't done it. They've no idea what it's like being a mum – they only ever see it completely objectively. And seeing motherhood objectively, without all these complicated feelings, makes it a doddle.

But it's not a doddle as you and me well know. It's tough, terrific, challenging, exquisite at times but definitely tough. And judgements being made about your mothering are tough to put up with. Particularly as becoming a mum makes you so sensitive.

There's nothing wrong with being sensitive. Sensitive is good in my book. Sensitive means you are intelligent – intelligent enough to care about things. Sensitive people make society a more caring and considerate one. We could do with more of that.

But it hurts sometimes. Comments from others can make you feel like you're being judged – and probably being judged as lacking. You don't seem to get judgements about being great – have you noticed?

More often you get comments from relatives and peers like; 'oh – haven't you weaned her yet, isn't she too old for breastfeeding?' (Hidden criticism).

Or; 'are you still at home – are you going to get a job?' (In other words being a mother isn't a proper job).

Or; 'I always did the housework before she woke.' (Suggestion you're lazy).

As a mum you can feel really sensitive to comments like these, and those from relatives are probably the worst; 'I always did it *this* way' – in other words you're doing it wrong. These remarks can be quite hard to take – I know – I've had them too.

The way to deal with them is to ignore them as much as you can. Because basically you don't *have* to see them as judgements. You don't *have* to make judgements about *yourself* based on these comments. You don't *have* to take other people's judgements on board and turn them into a comparison between you and them. Or make them into expectations.

You can decide not to. Ignore them instead.

To do that you need to build confidence so surround yourself with enough trustworthy people who don't make remarks like these to you, with other mums who boost your confidence not take it away. A good support network of mums who will be aware of your sensitivities and look after them. As you do for theirs.

Build yourself a support network you don't feel judged by. Interact with judgemental mums as little as possible. Take steps to make yourself a good mum by being a mum happy and confident with what you're doing. See your caring supportive friends. Talk to them about judgements – about comments from insensitive others. Share your concerns. Build each other up. Make a pact to support each other in being individual, in doing it your way.

That'll help you cope and manage the sensitivity that all good mums feel. As will being aware.

Being aware

Being aware of what's happening, being aware of these loaded remarks and how they affect you, is the way to step beyond them, to overcome them. To look at them, to keep them in perspective, to continue to be the kind of mum you want to be. The kind of mum you're happy with.

Remember; it is your right to mother in the way that's best for you and your child. Not necessarily in the way others are doing it.

A thought to remember about judgements:

Other people's comments and judgements are often reflections of their *own inadequacies – not yours*. If they didn't feel inadequate, they wouldn't be making comments! You don't have to take *their* inadequacies on board. They're not *yours*. You are *not* at fault because you're not doing it their way. Keep seeing their attitude as *their problem* – NOT yours. That's the strongest way to deal with it.

Questioning and being aware of what you do as a mother is important. There will be times you want to change what you're doing, when other people's advice works best, when others can help you see things in a different way. But it won't be *every* time. And *your* way is valid too. Balance and perspective are both important. Judgements are not. There is nothing particular you *ought* to be doing other than what you think is the right way to care for your child based on a balance between advice and what you think.

A little story

*While I was talking to friends about what to put in this book and researching ideas the same concern came up over and over again. This was that all mums wished they'd had the courage and awareness to mother in the way that was right for them. And not in the way that was **expected** of them. That's what would have given them a greater pleasure with their time of being a mum. Many of the expectations and judgements of others stole that pleasure away.*

I'm hoping that this book is going to raise your awareness of the many pitfalls which expectation opens before you – so that you can step round them and grow greater confidence and skill in your own way of being a good mum.

Following are some of the most influential expectations.

Traditional expectations

Tradition brings an expectation package that sticks to you like Super Glue if you're not aware of it.

Traditional expectations about motherhood go so far back, and we are all so subtly conditioned by them, that it's almost impossible to do anything different. Traditions are nearly as ingrained in our behaviour patterns as breathing.

Despite being a contemporary society, with contemporary views on the role of women, friends and I still found traditional little expectations shaping the way we looked after our children and acted as mothers.

It is just so hard to get away from. However intelligent, trendy, modern, self-aware and free thinking you are.

The best example is still the one about the housework and home making. That's the easiest traditional expectation to shape what you do. That's the one most women fall prey to; the thing most women end up doing because it is expected.

It might have been the tradition in your family for the woman to do all the domestic stuff but is that what *you* choose?

It might have been the tradition in your family for the woman to maintain a career and use child care and that might be expected of you, but is that what you *choose*?

It might still be the tradition in your house to expect the children to sleep in separate rooms but does that work for you?

The traditional way of parenting in your family might expect lots of 'discipline' to get kids to behave but is that the right approach for you and your child?

Whatever was traditional in your family can soon place expectations upon you, especially in the form of comments by other family members. Notice what's happening to you in the form of those expectations. Notice if you're behaving in the way that's expected of you or the way you choose to behave.

Traditions are fine as long as they are not expectations that are governing your behaviour without you making a conscious **choice**. Ending up doing what's expected rather than what you want makes you feel frustrated and resentful.

Choosing and deciding what kind of mother you want to be is what will give you the best chance of enjoying it. Recognise these expectations for what they are. Free yourself from them. Keep sight of what works for you and your child in your new little family.

A little story

Here's a typical story of how my traditional expectation ruined a perfectly good afternoon...I expected one afternoon to do some baking with my youngest, by then three years old. This was my idea of something a perfect mother at home with her kids would be doing. She being the inquisitive and independent character she is (and I should have known this if I'd stop to think), had her own agenda. She was much more interested in the feel of the flour, and spooning it, and slopping water into it and so on... Me, though, with my perfect expectation, pressed on with trying to make the cake, getting more and more stressed because it wasn't working out how I'd expected. Guess how it ended? With tantrums. From both she and I. It was an awful afternoon all round.

*Moral of the story: let expectations go and **see** what's really happening. If I'd seen what was really happening which was she having a great time playing with flour and water, instead of trying to maintain my unreal expectation, we would have all had a much happier afternoon. She with her messing would have been busy for ages and I could have had half an hour on the settee with a cuppa!*

Hope that story helps. Watch what you're doing and avoid my pitfalls.

Expectations about your child's stages

You are bound to have expectations about your child – what she will do and how she will behave, her development and so on - and so will others you come into contact with. It is easy to become anxious, embarrassed, stressed or distressed when these expectations are not met.

Just as everyone seems to have opinions about what sort of mother you should be, they all seem to have an opinion on how your child should be and when they should develop too.

There's nothing worse than being in a situation where your child is not doing something you expected and you're becoming wound up about it. Or not behaving how you expected her to behave and you're feeling bad about it.

It's inevitable that you expect certain milestones in your child's life to be reached at certain times. Anyone who's ever read advice will have unconsciously set times for certain events – like the first tooth perhaps or being able to use the toilet. And when it doesn't happen on cue they become BIG ISSUES.

Sometimes you may need to be concerned. *Mostly* you don't.

<u>A little story</u>

*My friends and I have discovered, having lived through most of these stages now with several children, that more often than not there's no need for concern at all. It's just each child is **individual**. That's just the way they're doing it.*

Once we stopped expecting these stages to be reached as per the website or baby manual, and instead allowed them to come in our child's own time, we felt so much easier. We stopped being overly concerned. Everyone was a whole lot happier. And often, in the end, it only amounted to a mere day or two, or a week or two in difference. It's only when you're waiting on it to happen with certain expectations that it becomes a Big issue.

Your child will not always develop on cue. Or per the media. Or the same as everyone else's. Or the same as your friend's.

So don't set time limits. Wait and see. Cut the expectations and you cut it being an issue. Free yourself from set expectations. All will happen in the end. You can't rush development.

(There's more on this issue in the next Tip-Bit).

Expectations about behaviour

Equally you can't rush the rate at which your child matures.

Rate of maturity affects your child's development and behaviour and ability and there's nothing you can do about it except give the guidance and encouragement you'll already be giving and let all expectation go. Time takes care of most things.

Expectation about behaviour is what causes mums the most anguish. Most especially if your child is not living up to expectations you may have had about that perfect biddable child who's never rude, and does what it's told.

Wouldn't we all like one of those? Well, actually, maybe not. They'd be pretty boring and lacking in spirit. I like spirit. I like character and individuality.

Trouble is; it's a handful.

We all have rosy pictures of how our child is going to be perfect. Because we're determined we're not going to be like those awful parents who shout, lose control, get wound up, horrible to our kids even. We're going to be loving and responsible parents who interact with our children in a humane and respectful way, thus showing them the correct way to behave, which they will of course adopt.

Go on – admit it – you had that expectation too. I did. My friends did. We nestled our perfect babies in their perfect new shawls against us and expected the perfection that every new life is to last.

Next thing you find yourself all bewildered by this wilful demonstrative child, who has a mind of its own, a personality of its own and a will power you've suddenly realised with panic is becoming stronger than yours.

Those initial expectations about perfect children with perfect behaviour shatter as they mature from being that perfect little new-born into little people in their own right. Little people who have characters and ideas all of their own.

And some of those characteristics take some getting used to. Most particularly when you're expecting perfect.

Expectations about our children's behaviour is *hardly ever* realistic. *But* we all fall into the trap of it. We're all just as shocked as you when your child says its first wilful 'NO'. When the first lie gets told. When your child first whacks someone else's. Or behaves like an absolute demon in company grabbing all the toys.

It's a shock. And embarrassing. But maybe if you expected it was inevitable then it would be a lot easier to bear. *Because it IS inevitable.* I'm afraid to tell you; that's what kids do.

Now, I'm not saying that behaviour is okay. Or desirable. Or something you'll want to encourage as a parent.

What I'm saying is that despite them being wonderful and you loving them desperately, *children are not perfect. They don't behave perfectly.* And all for the simple reason that they are growing and learning about behaviour and while they're doing that they make awful *mistakes*. What we need to do is release our expectations and remember that.

So often parents forget that simple truth.

You can easily forget that your children have a long way to go in their learning about behaviour, you forget that they are bound to get it *wrong* sometimes, you forget reality because you expected something different. And you can sense that those around you expected something different too.

Ignore them, keep demonstrating and explaining to your child what is desirable and be patient. Less fuss the better. Keep focussed on what you want to happen and it will come, but don't expect it to happen straight away.

Expectations at Toddler Group and other gatherings

You can often find yourself in these unhappy situations when you begin interacting at places like toddler groups.

Toddler groups, playgroups, nurseries, and gatherings like them, place a whole load of unrealistic expectation upon our children (and mums) that can easily cause distress.

Health visitors and other experts uphold toddler groups as the perfect way for mums to meet and the perfect way to integrate your child with others.

Far from perfect, I see it more like a nightmare of unrealistic expectations which can be quite difficult to deal with depending on the group.

Think about it: how can a collection of sociably immature toddlers, of an age when they're at their egocentric worst, who are used to the exclusivity with toys they get at home, be expected to integrate with others at the same stage? And even more unrealistic – be expected to *share* toys when they have no concept of what sharing is. If ever there was an occasion where expectations were totally unrealistic it's at toddler group.

Putting your child with a group of others likely to biff her and snatch the toys off her is not going to teach her how to become sociable. It's ludicrous.

It's also devastating when it's your child doing the biffing. Which is quite likely at some point.

You immediately think you're doing something wrong as a parent. You immediately feel ashamed and inadequate. You immediately feel judged.

And it happens all because of ridiculous expectation about children too young and as yet underdeveloped to be able to interact and communicate in a peaceful and sociable way with others also as underdeveloped as they are. Some do. Many don't.

Despite expectations toddler group is not always an ideal place for your children to learn how to integrate. Toddler groups are great for meeting other mums for networking and an oasis of company if you're feeling isolated. Great for finding other toys and stimulation. Great if your child is at the stage of wanting other children around.

But don't necessarily expect all children to like it or to learn socially acceptable behaviour in this climate. They need a lot of guidance and reassurance. Socialising your child with others often works better in a more intimate setting. And there's nothing wrong if your child doesn't want to share – all of us at some stage don't want to share. Expecting small kids to is idiotic. They simply haven't reached that stage yet. They come to it in time – their *own* time – through your guidance.

They learn about all this from integrating with *all* others, but *mostly* with others who are *older* – namely adults. For children to learn how to socialise they need to be in natural social settings (family gatherings for example or round a friend's house) where there's a mix of others, not simply a mass of other unsociable beings the like of which you get at toddler groups.

Many children don't even *enjoy* being with a noisy, threatening, intimidating group of others anyway *and there's nothing wrong with that*. I don't. Mine didn't when they were little. They are fine in company now and enjoy it enormously.

All children are different – I know I keep saying this but the expectation is that we seem to want them all the same. Some kids are loners. That's normal. Some kids are not. That's normal too. Some kids like being with others from the start. That's normal. Some don't – they take longer to enjoy the company of others. That's normal too.

(There's more on this in Tip-Bit No.7)

There is a sometimes an expectation for kids to enjoy mixing right from the start and that sets some kids and their mums up for misery if it's not right for them. You have a right to choice.

A little story

I didn't do toddler groups after a while. My kids hated it. I hated it. I saw it as a batch of expectations that were not matching reality. The reality was – they weren't ready for it - attending wasn't doing us any good. So I stuck with my intuition and didn't go. We mixed with lots of other mums in a more intimate way and my kids enjoyed lots of friends. We are not scarred for life not doing toddler groups. Come to that – we didn't do a lot of things thrust under our noses as the thing we should be doing with our babies and children – we made conscious choices instead. And I think we're still quite normal. The kids seemed to have turned out okay.

*However, thought I'd say that at the start when I did try them out, when **I** wanted some company, I met my best friend who is still my friend now twenty years later. But we spent more time round each other's houses and on outings than we did at groups.*

Take courage to steer your own path. Take courage to step out of what is expected into what you enjoy. And what makes you and your child happy. See the reality. Take the pressure off you and your child.

Dip into the groups that work well for you. Equally, you don't have to go just because everyone else is going. Other situations might suit you and your child better. Be aware. Research options. You're allowed to make choices.

Here's another story

We were visiting friends. Friends with tidy peaceful houses unused to the invasion of untidy un-peaceful children.

We sat in the tidy peaceful living room with our legs crossed tidily, toddler on the carpet in the centre (nothing to do – everything tidied away). We sat drinking our tea from precious cups all as stiff and uncomfortable with each other as cardboard cut-outs. Not knowing what to say. All staring at the toddler to avoid looking at one another and making remarks like 'isn't she cute?'

Talk about pressure!

The toddler of course felt it. Felt all these eyes everywhere she looked so, enjoying the audience, started to perform. I forget most of the 'performance' now except tea being knocked over and settees being leapt on and ornaments fiddled with until removed. But I remember the pressure. And I remember thinking; sod this! This is so unfair. There's all these adults in this room so uncomfortable with each other we've turned our attention on the child and then we expect her to 'behave' under all this pressure.

I got up and took her out into the garden where we could both let off steam.

I saw this happen so often. I saw so much pressure put upon small children – all children actually – simply to relieve our own adult inadequacies. I see expectation and reality not matching and the kids getting the brunt of it.

See if you can spot it in your gatherings – family ones are often the worst. Be aware of steam gathering and let the heat off expectations.

You're a mum. You're a parent and it's your responsibility to observe and to make decisions about what's good for your child. You're allowed to do what you think is right even if it's not necessarily what's expected of you.

Do what's comfortable for you – rather than what's expected. Do what you do out of love.

Self-fulfilling expectations

There is a point of view that you get what you expect. If you expect good things you get good things. If you expect the worst then you get the worst.

So how does this work for us if we're giving up high ideals and expectations? What will happen if we don't expect good behaviour, or things to go well? If we set no expectations surely we won't have good kids?

We can – what we need to do is change the pressure from too much *unrealistic* expectation into high hopes instead, and what is *real and achievable*.

It's the unreal expectations that do the damage. The unachievable ones. And the pressure for perfection they cause.

It's good to have high hopes. It's good to be working towards the best you can get. It's good to have the best expectations *for the circumstances* you and your child find yourself in.

But it's also good to *ditch them* if they're not right or not realised. It's better not to have them set in concrete; you only get devastated when they're not realised. It's good to remain open to change. It's important to keep real.

For example; happiness could be an expectation. But it wouldn't be realistic to expect happiness *all* the time. There will be hard times and down times. But there will be happy times too. Keep it all in perspective.

Another example; a loving relationship with your child could be a good expectation. But that doesn't mean it will necessarily be like that *all* the time. There will be conflict which you will need to manage in a calm, consistent and respectful way. A loving relationship *most* of the time is good enough. And is a better expectation.

Keep your expectations in balance. Remain aware, review often, think and decide what's important for you. Decide what kind of a mum you want to be to your child and be that, not merely what others expect you to be.

Thinking about expectations and how to help yourself avoid the pitfalls:

- Ask yourself what are you expecting?
- Are your expectations realistic and balanced?
- Watch out for the influence of the 'Should' Brigade.
- Look out for traditional expectations that may be affecting your choice.
- Remain with the stage of your child and don't expect things to happen at specified times.
- Don't expect your child or your parenting to be perfect.
- Be careful not to expect things to happen as they do on websites/baby books/magazines/media.
- Be aware of expectations others put upon you, including family.
- Choose to do what you want rather than what is expected.
- Be aware of expectations within groups and gatherings and institutions.
- Talk to other mums about expectations.
- Remember the loving bits.
- Forgive your child his mistakes.
- Remember to have high hopes - not unrealistic ideals.

Coping with all this stuff motherhood throws at you is no easy matter. Coping with the stress of everyone else's expectations – not to mention your own – is a tough job. You need to be strong. Strong enough to withstand the 'Should' Brigade. Strong enough to make choices that are right for you despite expectation. Strong enough to have the courage in your own convictions.

So where do you get all that strength from?

You get it from support. You get it from confidence, from believing in yourself. You get it from self worth. You get it from inner strength reserves. You get it from *really valuing* what you do. Valuing this worthwhile job of being a mum.

That's what the next chapter's all about.

Tip-Bit No 6: Ages and Stages

When should they be sleeping through the night?

When should they be sitting up?

When should they get their first teeth?

When should they be weaned?

When should they be out of nappies?

When should they be talking?

When should they be walking?

If you're reading this looking for advice as to the When of these events then the only thing I can tell you is that you're looking in the wrong book!

But the tip I do want to give you about the When Should is:

Generally speaking the When Should isn't important. It's another 'should' that wants discarding.

Understandably though mums get terribly anxious about how their infant is developing – me too – paranoia better describes it. And if there is one thing that makes mums even more anxious (if that's possible), then that is 'when' time frames (or 'shoulds'). Or age limits attached to these important milestones of development, which appear in advice.

Other mums and I who have been through it would like to lay your worries to rest by bringing something to your attention. If you look at the twenty or thirty rising five year olds, all lined up in their too big uniforms on their first day of school, you'll realise that the age they were before they all got their first tooth, ate their first meal, said their first word, or took their first steps actually is of *no consequence now what so ever*.

Mostly, it all happens in the end. Mostly, the When doesn't matter.

You can stop worrying.

But most first time parents do worry. In fact, all committed, caring parents worry, which is natural because obviously we all want our children to be OK, to be normal. We just need to try and keep it in perspective. And not let it become a worry of waiting, or a competition between you and other infants you know who've reached a stage yours hasn't.

Don't let it turn into a matching game between you and the developmental curves on websites or time scales written down as rough guides. Because these only are *rough* guides. Not gospel.

Lots of things happen developmentally in these first five years. Lots of exciting changes within a very short space of time. Obviously books and websites and those who study child development are bound to give some indication of when to expect these major events. They've seen it all before, it's all water under the bridge to them.

Trouble is, to us, watching and waiting with as much anticipation as when we've just phoned for a pizza, when the next major event isn't happening exactly as if it had been scheduled in the Olympics we begin to worry. The longer it goes on the more it gnaws away at us, the possibility that our child is 'backward'.

And, of course, we mums are mostly that besotted we're sitting there watching every move. And before we know where we are we're off down the clinic to ask 'is this normal?'

Most of us have peered intently into infant mouths when they're wailing looking for that first tooth. We might even have let the baby go on wailing a while just so we can get a good look while the mouth's wide open.

Most of us have chanted ourselves witless in front of the bouncy chair saying 'mama, mama, mama!' Even holding that favourite treat just a bit out of reach with a bit of subversive bribery.

Many of us have put that best loved toy just a bit too far away in the hope they'll get up and take a few steps.

And I bet most of us have worried ourselves to crying point, berating ourselves that we're useless parents, because our best friend's baby talked ages ago and ours is still only fluent in ga-ga.

Well, it's absolutely no good worrying. It changes nothing. There is absolutely nothing you can do except **wait**. Focus on what they **can** do.

And remember the staggering, amazingly obvious, much forgotten fact that

Children are not made on a factory production line.

They are *all different*.

If your infant is responsive, alert, awake and interested in what's going on around them then chances are they are absolutely perfectly normal, even though they may be taking longer than it says in the 'Every Mother's Guide To Child Development' to reach that milestone you're desperately waiting for.

Every child develops at a slightly different rate. And, as I've suggested, when you look forward in years as I appreciate it's very difficult to do when you're just starting out with these new adventures, the few days, weeks, months, year's difference between them all when they're tiny just evens out in the end.

<u>A little story</u>

Take mine as an example. They were chalk and cheese.

My first did everything to plan – just like it says in the advice (Yep - I read it too).

My second did everything differently. Her birth should have given me the clue, shouldn't it?

When it was 'time' for her to be walking she just didn't. I had an idea that she could; it was just that she got around a lot faster on all fours. One day she wore a romper suit that hung down and got in the way of her crawling fast so she got up and walked. She never looked back.

When it was time for her three and a half assessment the health visitor was concerned about her speech because she refused to talk whilst the health visitor was there. I think this was because she was busy getting everything out of the health visitor's handbag. I knew she could talk. She knew she could talk. But she wasn't going to perform for anybody so the health visitor had to come back – several times – before she was satisfied.

My daughter remains the same about things now – she does them when she's ready – when she has a need. That's just how she is. And no one could tell any difference between her and anyone else now she's adult.

If only we knew all this to start with. Wouldn't it be simple? And reassuring?

If only we could look ahead and see our cherished blobs all with teeth, all walking, all talking (do they ever stop?), all going to the loo properly, all grown, all perfectly normal. All the same as all the others at the football group or dance class.

While you're waiting on them these exciting events seem as if they're never going to come. Be reassured that they do all come, and with subsequent children, you'll stop hovering over them quite so much. Hard to imagine now isn't it? Have you heard the saying: 'a watched pot never boils'?

Try not to watch yours too much. And try not to worry. Because mostly you don't need to.

When you're at the time I am now you'll regret wishing time away so fast. It's a sad day when all these exciting little events are over and those precious little teeth all start dropping out and those confident young people walk out the door into their independent lives. The 'when' becomes insignificant and mostly totally unimportant.

What is important is to *enjoy* all the stuff happening *right now*.

*Enjoy the **now**!*

Relish every moment rather than worrying about its coming. I wish you many happy returns of these exciting milestones. Let them come when they will.

Chapter Seven

Mumworth

What is it all worth? All this work you do as a mum? All the dilemma and the decision making, all the labour and the toil, the role you now play, the time you spend with your child, the hard task of sorting it all out. The mountain of unending jobs. What is it all really, really worth? What is the value of it?

In answer to that question here's a fact that is so, so often overlooked:

PARENTS are SO IMPORTANT.

Because:

The *future of our world depends on the future of our children* and **parents** are responsible for that.

The work of caring for, raising, nurturing, encouraging, primarily educating and developing those children is what parents do. Therefore it is the most *worthwhile* work you could ever be doing. It is one of the most valuable positions in society that you could ever have. You will be influencing the future. Everyone's future.

How mums are worth it

Basically our children are a national treasure. Children and how they develop *will* govern the future; we'll be dead and gone and they'll be taking over and their children after that and so on....

So the people who care for them play a vital role. It's as straightforward as that.

Basically, in the hands of the *mums and dads lies the future of the human race*. Simply because the future of our society, of our race, of our planet, is perpetuated by our children and how they interact with it, so therefore it is also in the hands of the parents who are responsible for those children. And since it is we mums I'm focussing on here, it is therefore true to say that a part of everyone's future lies in *our* hands. It usually follows that what we do, our children will do. How we parent they will parent and so on...

Imagine for a moment who you're raising.

Imagine how you could be holding in your hands the initial care and development of the next Einstein, or the next scientist who will perhaps solve the problem of global warming, or the next Prime Minister who might be finally able to bring about world peace, the next consultant who may be able to find a cure for cancer, or the next person who can solve the problems of drug abuse, crime, unwanted pregnancies, and other flaws in our society.

Just imagine - you never know what your children will become. What a thought!

But it *is* true, isn't it? If you think about it like that – it must be – our children *are* the future. However big or small their contribution; in one way or another, they *will* be making a contribution. Our jobs as mums is to guide their contribution towards being a positive one.

For *equally important* are the less glamorous roles our kids might play like nurses or carers or teachers, cleaners or bin men, factory workers or farmers, creators of their own businesses. They are all an essential part of making our planet what it is. Every job our kids may do makes a contribution of some sort and it isn't any less valuable because it may be less well glamorised.

Yet the majority of society remains so blind to that simple staggering truth. And the worth of our children, the value of the mothers who devote so much of themselves, so much of their personal time and attention to caring for them, remains so criminally, and dangerously, underestimated.

I so feel for every mum out there. I feel for every grain of self that women give to be mums. For it's rarely appreciated how much is given. And lack of appreciation doesn't help mums to feel happy doing that giving.

It's important that mums have a sense of worth and happiness. It's important for our own sake, and it's important that our children are happy if they're going to thrive and become the valuable members of society that they could be.

More often they are a product of a society where happiness doesn't have its rightful and important place in our value system.

What does it matter? Why does happiness matter so much?

Why happiness matters and how society devalues mums

Happiness matters because happy people make up a society that is caring, respectful and good.

It matters because *the world's children* are important and to make a good contribution they need to be happy too.

It matters because your individual child is important and the work you do as a mother to raise your child is immensely valuable. So the *way you are* with your child will be much better if you are happy, you will be a better parent.

And it matters because mums and children shouldn't have to suffer this dreadful devaluation.

Mums can struggle to do what they feel is right for their children – for many of them do intuitively know what is right - because society doesn't support them in doing it.

Mums shouldn't have to struggle to hold their heads up in a society which continues to make the same blinding mistake; the same dangerous mistake of undervaluing mums and children, of not rating a mother's work highly, or rewarding that valuable work.

I think we have a society that doesn't even rate children highly or even see their potential for the survival of the planet and the human race.

Instead we have a society that politically professes to care, but in reality totally devalues the role of parents and discriminates against mothers who are the backbone of those children.

Society does this by creating a value system where greed is greater than need, where a higher income has more prestige than a valuable or humane contribution, where image is more important than goodness and honesty. And where materialism is huger than happiness; i.e., money is more important than love.

Since a mum's work is all about all of those things; all about satisfying need, developing goodness in their children, following a vocation to be a mum thus setting aside their opportunity to generate an income or contribute to business for a while, and best of all; nurturing happiness, they are therefore involved in nearly everything society fails to rate as valuable.

Not a happy situation.

Sadly, it is a sickening truth that women with children are discriminated against in the workplace if they rate those children as more of a priority than business. (So are men with kids for that matter).

Work wise mums are often discriminated against for being weak-willed, distracted, uncommitted, unemployable, mentally inept and generally a dodgy investment.

They are viewed by society in general as if they can contribute nothing except in a domestic capacity, be nothing more than a nuisance with a buggy and a pest in a restaurant if you come in with a child. And are sometimes regarded as a valueless, voiceless, insignificant, unimportant bunch of hormones, with low status in the business community, little true respect and with as much support and reverence as a city pigeon. Here's proof;

A little story

I've been glared at if my child is creating a fuss in a cafe, tut-tutted trying to get the buggy through a shop doorway and blocking the way for a while, looked down on for breast feeding in public even though I did it so discreetly no one could see anything. I was also asked 'Do you have a job?' as if the job I did as a mum was clearly not enough.

None of these things would have happened if society in general valued children and mums and the work they do. It demonstrates a total lack of respect.

And the biggest sign of disrespect and devaluing of our children comes through society believing it is acceptable to mass produce them down a factory line like herd animals as happens through schooling, and exclude the valuable role of parents from their education.(See my other books for further understanding).

And probably those who suffer all this lack of respect the most are single mums.

That *is* what a lot of mums have to put up with. Total devaluation of their important job of giving time to nurturing their child's development.

It's shocking. It's sad. But I'm afraid it is true – you don't have to look far or too deeply to see it. You'll no doubt have come across it.

This is all a bit negative and mumhood certainly isn't like that for the most part. But I wanted to bring it to your attention, to the world's attention, so that maybe something could be done about it.

It would be wonderful if we could turn that around. And begin to change attitudes. We can make a start by being aware of the way *we* think about it then maybe others will follow.

A more valuable perspective

What if you thought about it this way; what if you were to mother your children as if they *were* the next Einstein or David Attenborough perhaps? What if you *knew* at the start that they could be? Wouldn't it make a difference?

Well, that is exactly what you *can* do. It is exactly how you can *value* your role as a mum. Because, although you might not *exactly* be raising the next Einstein, *you are* raising another member of our future community who can make *just as valuable a contribution however big or small – it still matters*.

Acknowledge that:

ALL children make a contribution in some form to the next society.

YOUR CHILD will make just as important a contribution as any other.

YOUR work as a MUM is an immensely worthwhile contribution too.

The value of children

Your child is precious. You don't need me to tell you that. But perhaps she is more precious than you think – in ways you hadn't thought of before.

If, for arguments sake, we took for granted what I just said above, that you knew beforehand that your child was going to be another important scientist or someone similar, how would you feel? How would you treat your child and your time with her, how would you raise them then?

Einstein or not your child *can* contribute something great. He or she doesn't have to be a genius, make millions or be someone famous to do that.

Small caring responsible acts may not get media coverage, *but they are just as great*.

A humane individual, who is caring of, and responsible for the earth and the people on it, can spread caring ideas around the people they come up against. They, together with others like them, can make up a group. This humane caring group together with another group who are the same form a community, which together with another community form a society that is humane and caring, and so it goes on. A humane and caring society can improve the quality of our culture so much.

What a difference your child, all our children, can make in this way.

Your child has the *potential to make a contribution* like that. Your child has the potential to do great things with the right example and the right education. And when I say education I'm not talking about the mind-numbing qualification-getting that takes place in schools. (Check out my other work). I'm talking about the education your child gets from *you*. The learning that takes place in your home right now, with you, which is nothing to do with reading or writing or maths.

It is learning about how people look after each other, how to be respectful, considerate and kind, how to be responsible for the effect that their own actions have upon others and the environment. (Their primary environment being the home).How to be responsible for one another. How to understand others, be tolerant of their differences, how to get along, how to communicate, how to care. And of course how to love, how to be happy.

These simple things will be what make your child great. These things, started at home with you, will ripple out into the community. These small acts will make your child's contribution great as he grows. And that *will* matter and make a difference.

Your child can make such a valuable contribution by being a good person just as you make a difference being a good mum. Your child *is* valuable. *Right now. However small.* It starts here.

That's why it's so important to treasure our children, treasure the time we devote to them, because there's no telling what they may do so we need to give it some attention. We want their contribution to be positive and certainly not negative. Your positive attitude, your example of value, is what helps it to be so.

It is important that you regard your child as if, however small, they are equally as important as Einstein. Your children are precious – not only to you, but to the community, to the future. And *your attitude* about that matters. Your attitude will help change things.

The value of mums' work

So, consequently, each little job you do looking after your child, who will one day be making a great contribution, is worth it.

All the care, consideration, nurturing, understanding, love, tolerance, communication, education, it's all valuable. It all demonstrates to your child the point of caring for one another, for the wider community, for the earth. It demonstrates *value*. And for your child to make their own contribution in this way they will need to have it demonstrated to them.

That's what *you* are doing being a mum. Each little thing you do – however small, domestic or insignificant, *matters*. It's *all* important.

You are the one your child is learning from right now. His learning is very close to home – right under his very nose in fact.

All the caring for his clothes, her room, his house, the people in it, might just seem like unending domestic drudgery to you. (And I agree – it is sometimes – it's not something I enjoy, and in no way am I advocating you do a lot of it). But for your child this is his way of learning about caring. Of learning about being responsible for his world – his world being right at home at the moment. But these acts of caring and looking after are going to expand into the wider environment one day – and that's why it matters.

Seeing someone do it – feeling someone do it for them – being encouraged to contribute – these are all the ways your child learns to be caring too.

Taking that responsibility for a caring world lies at *everyone's* door, not just the mothers', but it's often the mums who it falls to. The care of your child, his home and the immediate things around him is your child's first reference to caring for others and the things in our world and that's what your work is demonstrating as you go through the tedium of tidying, managing, washing, cooking, recycling. It's all an education of care and responsibility which your child will hopefully practice himself and take out into the world and demonstrate to others.

Now, in no way do we need to make a big deal of it. This is just to show how the domestic stuff *does* have a value, it *is* worthwhile. It needs to be kept to a minimum and in proportion to other things – but it is important. It is as important as work outside the home.

Seeing work taking place outside the home is part of your child's education too, or work generating an income – some people do this at home. Children need to understand about this work, about working to support oneself, about income, about taking responsibility to do that independently and all that stuff. But for now, their world is quite small and that's something they'll understand more of later. For now, seeing how it takes work to create a home and a life is just as important.

All those small trivial acts that you do have a worth. They show care. They show you care for things. They show how value is placed. Builds values too. And showing how you care for your child will contribute to making them feel loved. Everyone feels happier if they feel loved.

It may be taking up a lot of your time, but it's worth it because of the example it sets. Never underestimate the value of what you do for your child in the home. It's SO important.

The value of your time

I've said that each small task you do for your child is valuable. Therefore each small moment you spend doing it is valuable too – it is time well spent. Because each one of these small moments – however trivial they seem to you - contributes to your child's feeling of *worthiness*. And that's what we need; children who feel worthy and valued.

Children who feel valued are more likely to contribute something great than children who don't. That's why spending time on them is important.

And that's exactly why the concept, which some parents use, of 'quality time' utterly stinks.

It stinks because as I've demonstrated *all* time spent around our children *matters*. And often, it is the most trivial times of all – which you may not think of as quality – which matter the most. Like being around when they're ill for example. You may not be doing anything particular with them at all – but you're *there*, and that *matters to them*. Being around *not* doing jobs is actually more important to them than even those jobs you do described above. It shows them that it matters to you that you're there just *because of them*. That tells them that *they matter* to you.

The idea of 'quality time' also stinks because it suggests that we are too busy ninety percent of the time to bother with our children which is a horrendous concept in itself. It also implies that if we invest in ten percent of 'quality' time it will make up for it.

It won't. It's not the way of things. *All* those itty-bitty bits of time are important. Especially to a child.

The notion of 'quality time' further stinks because it doesn't exist in the real world of children. For time with a child that is of quality usually cannot be scheduled, it is spontaneous. It can rarely be planned; when it is, it often goes wrong. Like with me and the cake-making!

'Quality time' is an adult concept, for the convenience of adults, to fulfil adult guilt and which totally overlooks small children's needs to *have you there*. Often without even interacting with them. That's what matters to children.

Children's needs are random and totally unpredictable in terms of 'when'. They need you to be there when *they* need you to be there, not when *you* need/want to be there. Obviously we can't be there all of the time to the exclusion of everything else, that's not what I'm talking about, it's not good anyway. I'm just illustrating how time with them, however mundane, is of value.

And finally, *we wouldn't even need the concept of 'quality time' if we truly valued our kids and all the time we spent with them – even the not so good times.*

Yes – the concept of 'quality time' stinks. Children are more important than that. *All* the time you give to be with your child is valuable. You might not think so – but it is.

Never underestimate your time spent.

Time's worth is hard to measure and in a culture obsessed with valuing only that which can be measured or scored it is easy to underestimate. But your attitude of placing value on time spent with your child will start to change that.

Look at it this way; you place value on time spent working to earn. What we need to do is to place equal value on the time spent raising a child.

A priceless work ethic

Your time spent at work brings you an income – that is valuable, essential obviously. But your time spent *not* at work is equally valuable.

The work (and big business) ethic in our culture, where you're measured by your income, has become too strong – too strong a trend. And so often it is just about trend. Because of the trend to be seen earning at all hours, time spent on *each other* has suffered as a consequence. It's not seen as trendy to be spending time with your child. Spending time with your child does not come across as upbeat, professional or worthy as earning.

We need a new trend. One that recognises the value of work with small children.

Time spent earning is required – it goes unsaid we need an income. But never forget that time spent being there for your child is required too, in fact it's ***priceless.***

Our culture has lost its way with valuing time spent on each other. In its race for money, media and materialism we've sacrificed the importance of *love* and *family*. In the race, race, race for ever increasing income (or is that image?) and virtual connectivity we have abandoned spending time on connecting for real and *building relationships.*

This is evident not only in the way we raise families now, but in the caring professions too; nurses; teachers; doctors; care workers. They all have had to abandon giving time to human beings because they have business targets to meet.

We may be more connected via social networking, but this also allows us anonymity which does nothing for caring and building relationships as problems with Facebook 'relationships' and people not having to be accountable for unpleasant remarks has shown. As well as finding us new relationships it can also damage relationships. We have to pay more attention to the way we build relationships and giving people time.

If there was one single thing that would solve many of the problems our society faces, that would cure many illnesses and ease suffering, that would lessen crime and build community, that would raise the standard of our children's education drastically, it would be the *recognition* of the *value* of ***people** time.*

Many of society's problems are founded in lack of *people time*, in poor relationships, in relationships suffering because there's no people time devoted to them. Relationships between parent/child, partners, friends, communities, cultures. Building these worthwhile relationships takes *time with a person*. It's such a valuable investment but it's not recognised as such. Even less so as we increasingly do away with face to face time and use technology instead.

A little story

When our children were babies there was an advert on the telly that promoted some of the first mobile phones. The story was about a mum at work late, but it didn't matter because if she had a mobile she'd still be able to read her child a story – down the phone – even though she wasn't there. As if that was all that mattered. It didn't matter that she wasn't present because she now had a phone. And everyone in the story was happy with that? Another indication of how little our culture values giving people time by being physically there.

Our children, all children, need people time – parent time. They need it at home when they're young more than anything. You never get that time back. It is priceless.

Every moment you spend is worth something. Perhaps it is worth more than work – only you can decide that. Perhaps you can manage on less coffees and take-away meals so you can have more people time. You can help create a new priceless work ethic of spending time with your child instead of on un-necessaries. We have more choice on that than we think.

The value of love time

One of the most valuable things you demonstrate as you labour at all those irritating, time consuming little jobs as you care for your child, and give of your time to do so, is *love*.

The power of love is something else that is widely underestimated.

It can heal hurts, develop confidence, beat blues, encourage independence (rather than the other way round as people tend to think), ease ailments, mend mishaps, give comfort, and best of all make your kid feel happy.

Love is an important part of the happiness package. They go hand in hand. Your kids need love in order to thrive.

The value of your job of being a mother is rooted in love.

In fact, it's a labour of love being a mum. Sometimes it seems all labour and no love. It seems to be all toil, all work, all conflict, as your child grows and exercises will-power, or whirlwinds the house, or revels in muck.

All the labour you do to cope with it is all valuable. But keep it in perspective.

LOVE is the most valuable thing of all. NOT the labour. Don't let the labour waste your loving bits.

Love is demonstrated by your *interaction* with your child. By your relationship with her. Not by tidiness, cleanliness, an expensive home or anything material. Your child knows how much he's loved by how you *behave* towards him. It's that simple.

By your interest, attachment, time spent, this is what demonstrates whether he's a priority or not. And kids *know* that. They are not fooled by excuses – or by gifts as much as they love them and we love giving them. They are not a replacement for the value of love. Your demonstration of love teaches a child how to love others too.

Love takes time and investment. It's the best one you'll ever make. It's more valuable than anything else for the time being. For this short time while you have young children. It ends so quickly and other priorities can take over again.

The love you bring to the way you raise your child is something *no amount of income can match.* And this wonderful gift you have, that so many others are sadly denied - a child - is also something that *money can't easily generate.*

Your work as a mother has a value *higher* than income or anything material.

Your work as a mum is SO valuable. And your child's and everyone's future depends on it.

The value of generating happiness

I've already said; happy people make a happy society. Happy people are generally nice to one another. And that's what makes a better society.

That's why happiness is SO important.

Your happiness is important. Your child's happiness is too. Your child picks up vibes easily. He knows when things are not happy. Keeping yourself well looked after, rested, relaxed will make him as happy as it does you. Happy children are more co-operative. Motherhood is lovely all round if everyone's happy.

Keeping your child happy is not about giving in to every demand. That's not what I'm talking about. There are always incidents, circumstances, and problems that disrupt everything.

And we can't keep everything happy all the time. But keeping motherhood light – that is what makes a big contribution towards everyone being happy.

Valuing your time spent with your child, feeling the magnificent worth of your mum work, valuing your precious child, seeing this time as important, as a worthwhile investment of energy, *really feeling your worth,* that will all contribute to your happiness in what you do – even if some of it you don't want to be doing right now. And there'll probably be quite a few bits like that.

People who are happy develop well, learn well, stay healthier, live longer, are the best kinds of people to be with.

That's where the value of happiness lies. That's why it's important to give time to develop it whenever you can. For you. For your child. And consequently for everyone you and your child come up against.

I cannot reiterate enough the value of truly appreciating the worth of what you do and how that feeling will contribute to the happiness of your new family.

Happiness doesn't always come easily. It needs working on sometimes. We can work on it by maintaining a positive attitude. By being careful with what we're thinking. If your thinking becomes a bit negative, which at times it's bound to, just keep *affirming* to yourself, especially if it's not being confirmed from your community, that what you do now has *worth.*

It is valuable.

And *it is important.*

It will have a big impact on your life.

And an impact on the wider community.

Don't forget you very well may be raising the next Darwin, the next Kate Middleton, the next Stephen Hawkins or even Adele or a new Bob Geldof. Whoever it is – just act as if you are. Attach that kind of importance to what you do.

This time will change. It will change faster than trends. Your child will change. So will your time together.

For this period in your mumhood your happiness probably revolves very much around the interaction with your child that I've been talking about. It needs to be good for you to enjoy it. So let's look at that next.

Before we do, remember what you're worth as a mum.

Thinking about worth:

- Remember that everyone's future lies in the hands of our children.
- YOU have an enormous impact on that which is why what you do is SO valuable.
- Value your child – they are going to make a contribution to the world.
- Value each little moment spent.
- Value each little job you do however insignificant.
- Attach importance to LOVE.
- Attach importance to HAPPINESS.
- Relax, keep light, keep rested, enjoy.
- Remember all the reasons why MUMS ARE WORTH SO MUCH.

Tip-Bit No 7: Social Interaction and Other Illusions

There is always a lot of pressure on new mums to get their child interacting with others as soon as possible. As if it was some kind of essential and pleasant experience we're missing out on.

"Are you taking him to the clinic?" people ask as you reel from the birth, stitches still throbbing.

"Is she going to start toddlers soon?" This when you're still at the stage you can't get dressed in the morning let alone dress up to go out.

"Is she interacting with others?" "When is he going to nursery?" They enquire in a tone of voice that suggests that you 'should' be seeing to it. No one ever puts it the other way round; "You're not going to toddlers already are you?"

There is something you should know about social interaction among small children – just so you don't have unrealistic expectations and can release any pressure you might feel;

Social interaction among young children is not always the pleasant and relaxing experience it's held up to be.

Yet, as mums, we are led to believe that we need to get our infants used to company and if our tiny child is not calmly and happily interacting successfully with others then it is generally considered to be our fault, that we're doing something wrong, or that there's something wrong with our child.

Well, to put your mind at rest right now; that's rubbish - a total illusion. A misconception our culture seems to perpetuate. And worth examining to get at the reality.

The reality is that in many instances; grabbing, hitting, pushing and shoving, biting and kicking, hair pulling and scratching, tantrums and rage are much more common than social skills among small beings. (Actually we could probably bring to mind a few adult beings who have also resorted to that behaviour!)

But that behaviour is all perfectly normal, understandable and occasionally does happen among normal young kids.

When you consider the stage young children are at, how inexperienced and unskilled they are as yet, how could we expect it to be any different? When you consider that these children are at the stage where they want what they want and will risk danger and death to get it, you can see how it would be.

This is the way nearly all small kids are. This is all quite normal. There's nothing wrong with your child if this is what they're doing. It's not your fault.

So you can heave a big sigh of relief. You and your child are normal – you'll want this behaviour to change and it will, but be patient while you educate them to do it differently.

All mums who've been through it know this. Our own mums all know it. Grannies all know it. They all say; 'they'll grow out of it'.

But you can be made to feel that you must do the social interaction bit with your kids, whether they're ready for it or not, or you're failing as a mum and risk scarring them for life. I want to reassure you that this is not the case.

I repeat: no small child is capable of interacting in a way that is not egocentric. They mostly can't help it, they're just not grown up enough. Their world as yet revolves around them.

Look at it this way. You take your toddler along to this room full of wonderfully, exciting, tempting, attractive toys that his little eyes latch onto like yours do on chocolate éclairs. Then you tell him the bad news; *he has to share*. We all know that the majority of pre-school kids find sharing difficult, if not impossible. That's just the developmental stage they're at.

So it follows that if ever there was a potential battleground then putting a load of selfish, possessive, egocentric toddlers all together in one room to share toys is it.

Toddler groups and the like are great places for mums and children to get to know one another. To get them out of the house. To help them become less isolated. To make new friends if that's what they want. (Not forgetting some don't).

But let's not forget that *that is what they are for*. For kids to have a play with others if they want to (occasionally it works – for a while), and for mums to get to know each other, share concerns, offload worries, find support, to detach themselves from their little cling-ons for a moment in a confined space and have a breather.

But *it is not necessarily an ideal place for young children to develop their social skills*. Not if mums want to ignore their kids for a time while they're distracted and drink coffee as mums in their right mind want to do.

But the illusion of toddler groups sold to us leads us to believe that it is. That it's a social education – it isn't.

We are also made to feel that, if it is our kids that are doing the biting, hitting and shoving that day, then our kids are social misfits who should know better.

They're not.

Conversely, if your kid's the one crumpled on your knee with his hands grasping your neck and his face buried in your bosom, then you're made to believe that you're a soft mum, you need to take a firm hand, toughen your kid up or he'll never survive.

You don't.

These are all illusions we need not believe.

Looking beyond the illusion; in the first instance just putting kids in this sort of environment, where there are temptations beyond endurance is asking for a fight.

In the second instance, no little being in their right mind would want to get out into the fray of twenty little kids fighting over toys. Would you?

Thirdly, many kids find noise and crowds intimidating and will take some time to get used to them – if ever.

Toddler groups, play groups, nurseries etc are great for mums to get together or have a break, interact with other adults, maybe create a little distance for you and your child at times. But they are not really a lesson in socialisation, so you don't need to go for that reason, even if you want to go for others.

You are allowed to make the decision that's right for you and your child.

If you don't want to go to functions, then don't. You don't have to go to the nursery if you don't want to. You don't have to go to toddlers if you don't want to and it's not working for you or your child. And your kid doesn't *have* to go to Playschool. Or any institution you and they aren't happy with, come to that. School included, (but that's another book).

Be brave enough to do what *you* think works for you. Read up about it. Sift through advice. Ask friends. Do what your intuition tells you is right for you and your child, do what you and your child are comfortable with – not just the thing others think you should be doing because that's what they did. And don't let others pressurise you into believing that socialisation comes by forcing kids into groups. That just doesn't work.

It doesn't work for the obvious reason that children do not learn socially acceptable behaviour by being with large groups of other children *who have no idea* how to interact themselves, and are not at a stage where they can interact amicably or skilfully.

So how do children learn how to interact and be sociable?

They learn from people who *do* have social skills.

They learn to socialise by being with sociable members of the human race – not with anti-social ones. Other small kids come into the latter category.

Children learn to socialise through the social interaction we all have, all the time, naturally, with our peers, our family, our friends, in the course of our everyday lives. On outings, at the shops, parties, family occasions, down the market, in the park, celebrations, community events, where there is a better proportion of *all* members of the human race, old and new, not just small, socially unskilled ones.

These occasions provide a much better education and demonstration of social rules and behaviours than twenty other two year olds who have no idea about that sort of thing yet, or any organisation where there are large, unnatural clusters of children. Schools included.

The idea that children learn how to interact from clusters of others at the same stage is a ridiculous idea. An illusion that we've been miss-sold for years, making us feel guilty and sometimes inadequate if we don't buy into it.

It's best not to worry about it.

Give your child some time. Value the stage they're at. Their behaviour will change. Stop worrying yours is so shy she keeps her hat pulled down over her eyes. That's exactly what one of mine did and she loves talking to folks now. Stop worrying that yours is a brave little bruiser who goes for what she wants – that kind of assertive personality will pay dividends later in life when it's expressed with more skilful moderation.

Sometimes, more focussed groups, like music or exercise/dance group for little ones, can be better and feel more comfortable as they tend to be more directed than the play mayhem of Toddlers. It might work better for you.

Or just mix, at this stage, with carefully chosen friends where it is a positive and warm interactive experience for you and your child. Mix with mums who understand the stage your child's at, mums who are honest and sympathetic. Not mums who think they've got the only angel.

Unfortunately, interaction between some mums can soon become a competition as fierce as football. It is very difficult to be in the company of other mums without this happening. Especially if one child will share and one will not. One's a hitter and the other isn't. One hands over toys peacefully and the other fights for them. It's all very disconcerting. Choose carefully.

And remember that whichever child we are blessed with, and we are blessed – it isn't *all* our own doing – and however irritating, difficult or downright embarrassing your child is when with others, we perhaps need to remember that *all kids are different, all kids develop at different rates*.

And remember also to allow our child to be themselves as much as possible whilst continually encouraging consideration for others, consideration for possessions, consideration for the environment. Your example will eventually show them the worth of that – the point that consideration makes you a nice person to be with and that brings friendship rewards throughout life. But have some empathy and understanding of this difficult learning process your child is going through and have faith in the fact that they are not there yet but *will get there in the end*.

All we need to do, as we show them the right way to interact with others, is to never stop loving them for what they are.

They see the way we interact with others, they see the way our family and friends do, they learn all the time. It comes naturally. I don't believe we have to force interaction on them, or put them in distressing situations, which they are unready for, in which they continually fail. We need to wait. Encourage. Wait. Encourage.

If there's any forcing to be done, perhaps it's us mums who have to force ourselves out of the house and to meet friends once in a while, but not the kids.

Some of us grow up to be party animals. Some do not. Some are go-getters. Some are not.

We all grow and change constantly however old we are. You are growing and learning and changing as you further your comprehension about what it is to be a mum.

So is your child.

It all works out in the end!

Chapter Eight

Mother and Child

I believe that for most of us, for most of our lives, our happiness is founded in one basic thing.

That thing being warm, loving, satisfying *relationships*.

That's all. Not our income. Not our nice homes. Not our clothes, our possessions or our cars. Not even our work, however much we love it, and anyway relationships are always tied up with that too.

No, those things are add-ons like Apps really and our happiness requires and is dependent on something much more fundamental. It's dependent upon our deep human need for nurturing relationships; for love. Both to give and to receive.

That's what makes us happy. It's that simple.

Well – the idea is simple anyway. The implication of it is a bit more complicated.

It gets complicated because all our relationships are governed by different personalities and by different circumstances, which are not something we can always manage as we would like.

Being a mum, certainly being a happy mum, is just as dependent on relationships as any other part of your life. Your happiness is bound to be affected by the relationship you have with your child as they grow beyond babyhood. And what makes most mums happy will be establishing a good one.

So what's a good relationship anyway? And how can you foster one?

You're probably thinking that a good relationship is all to do with you being a good mum. It is a bit – but not only – and it might turn out to be different from what you're thinking anyway.

Being a good mum to your child

When we think about being a good mum we tend to think about our provision. We tend to think it's about what we provide as we look after our child, i.e. clothes, food, warmth, shelter, toys and treats, outings and birthday bashes. We tend to think we need to *provide things* in order to be a good mum. But that's only one small part of it; the simpler part, in my view.

You could live in a tumbled down shack in the middle of nowhere, have little money, and only be able to provide the very bare necessities but you can still be a good mum, a brilliant mum.

How come?

Because the larger part of what makes a good mum is not only made up of what we tangibly provide. It's all about other stuff as well. Being a good mum is all about the first word of this section – of this sentence. It's about *being*.

It's about the way you are, the way you behave towards your child.

But before I elaborate on that there's something very important you need to understand while you're thinking about being a good mum: *Being a good mum is not about being perfect.*

Being a good mum is more about being some of these things as much as we can:

- being fair
- being honest
- being open
- being loving
- *being realistic*
- being respectful
- being interested
- being attentive
- being considerate
- being committed
- being caring
- being on your child's wavelength
- being on your child's side
- being yourself too.

Now, you'll notice that *being realistic* is in Italics on the list. Why? Because it's SO important to remember that, realistically, *you are human*. You have failings. You are not perfect and you can't be all these things, all of the time, without a blip. No one can. I can't. No other mums I know can.

We all lose it, we are all horrible sometimes, we all lose touch with being kind, caring and considerate and loving when the little ones have wound us up to a pitch. We have all treated our children without respect or honesty in those dire moments when we've lost it. We've all been unfair and sometimes totally uninterested and more concerned about just being left alone. Losing it some of the time does not make us bad parents.

It just happens to all of us at some point. It's not good – but we can't help it. We're not perfect. We're only human.

But what we can do for most of the time is to be aware of *being as well behaved towards our children, as we would expect them to be,* as much as we can. That's how you can be a good mum.

That's also where respect comes in.

Building good relationships

Building good relationships is *all* about *mutual respect.*

Some parents don't seem to get what respect is. They think it's to do with authority. It isn't. That's a by-product.

Respect in a parent/child relationship is quite simple really; it's taking care. Demonstrating care and consideration towards your child as you would like demonstrating to you. And mutual respect is respect that they show for you *because* you've shown it to them. Kids don't always get it right; they're learning. But they learn most from how you behave so you have to be consistent.

This is very, very important. Respect is the foundation of your good relationship.

Adults tend to forget – children are people too, even if not adult. And as people they deserve the same respect as any other human being. But do I see that? Not always.

Sometimes I see children ignored when they are speaking – just because they are children. Sometimes I see children bullied into things they don't want to do just because they are smaller. Sometimes I hear children being told things that are totally untrue and dishonest just so adults can get their way, e.g. 'don't do that or a policeman will get you'. Sometimes I see adults pretending they're listening when really their mind's elsewhere. Sometimes I see children being treated as if they are totally boring and irritating, yet some adults can be equally boring and irritating but because they are adults we pay them attention. You see what I mean?

Some adults have one set of rules for children and another set of rules for themselves. How unfair is that? This is not respect.

Now, I know there are circumstances where children and adults need treating differently. But it doesn't therefore mean that children need to be treated with *less respect* than they deserve just because they're not adult yet.

Children who are treated with respect give back respect because they learn to treat others from the way they are treated. As I said, it's mutual.

In fact, *all* parts of relationship building should be mutual.

All those things in the list above – they're all mutually inclusive. Just as you are being caring, considerate, honest, etc., then your child will learn from that and reciprocate. That's what you need to encourage. And that's what being a good mum entails. You *being* a certain way with your child. That's how you take responsibility for being a good parent and that's how your child learns to be a good person too.

You won't be perfect but you will learn and change too. But being this caring respectful and good mum will build a lovely relationship. And that's what will contribute to your happiness as a mum and that contribution will eventually spread out into the world.

Some things you can do with your child to help you grow a good relationship

This is all going to take time. This is all going to take up your energy. There is no way round it. But it matters. Relationships aren't built with a few quick minutes attention and a lot of promises. They need big input.

But it is worth it. The reward will be unparalleled – it will build you an unparalleled relationship that will last for life. This is so worth investing in.

Here are some of the ways you can invest, they might seem obvious but can soon get overlooked in our busy, busy lives:

- *Listening*. That is; looking your child in the eyes and giving them time to tell you what they have to tell you, not continuing to watch Eastenders.
- *Talking*. That is; telling your child things about you, about your day, about the world, that demonstrates that you value them enough to share this information.
- *Allowing time* for two-way conversations – however trivial they seem to you. After all, we put up with plenty of trivial small talk from other adults.
- *Playing* with them with their toys. That is; getting down on the floor and really getting involved, asking them about *their* toys, not taking over the game and doing it your way or seeming to play while still watching Eastenders.
- *Going out together*. That is; for the outing itself and for an opportunity to interact, not just dragging them round Asda while thinking about last night's episode of Eastenders. (Okay – you don't watch Eastenders but you know what I'm getting at!)
- *Respect* their opinion. Show them you value it. Listen to it. Let them have opinions of their own. Don't cut them down if they are wrong. Put your point of view but not always as the right one.
- *Respecting* that they have intuition too – you can't be crying all over the place and say 'nothing's the matter.' It's dishonest. It doesn't work. Instead you can say you're tired, or unwell, or sad and, importantly, you'll feel better later. But don't fob them off when there's something clearly wrong. Not if you want them to trust you.
- *Read* them stories *any* time. Or look at books together. All children love stories and books, non-fiction too. It's always something you can do together.
- *Tell them why* or why not in answer to their questions, at whatever age, even if you have to be selective about information. They will learn to review their opinions if they know the why.
- *Credit them with ability*. Allow them to do things – show them you trust them to do things. Children are capable of doing a lot more than most adults realise.
- *Love them unconditionally*. Do things for them unconditionally. Don't always have a proviso. I hear so many adults saying 'yes you can when you've…' or 'alright but…' or 'okay then, if…' It

can soon become a habit. Say an unconditional 'yes!' as much as you can.
- *Don't be afraid* to say no, but when you do say no turn it into something positive. Like 'that's not a good idea because… but you could do this…' And only say 'no' and 'don't' when it really matters. Be economical with those words.
- *Give them respect* as you would any other person/adult. Sometimes I ask myself; would I have said that to my partner? Would I have behaved like that to another adult? We're none of us perfect. We can all slip into less than respectful behaviour towards our small beings. We just need to be aware of it.

These small ways can help you towards establishing a happy relationship between you and your precious child.

Because *that's what matters*. For you. For them. For the wider world.

Your child

Of course, your relationship with your child is not only dependent on you. It's also dependent on *them* too.

Something else to remember while you're building your relationship with your child: *Every child is different. Every relationship with every child will be different.*

Just as children come in wildly different packages – different hair, different eyes, different growth rate, different, height, etc. - so too do they come in wildly different personalities, strengths, weaknesses, idiosyncrasies. And this makes for lots of different relationships.

Your relationship with your child is going to be unique to you both. It is not going to be the same as anyone else's. It is not something you can predict. It's best not to expect anything. It's best just to go with whatever is happening at the time. And remember that however your child is, their behaviour will probably be moulded on how *you* behave and that's what you need to pay attention to most.

There are some children with special difficulties who find it hard to pick up on social and behavioural clues and learn from them. But mostly children do learn how to behave and interact in an acceptable way from your example. *Eventually.*

Be patient

The trouble is while you're getting to that time *eventually* you really do have to remember to be *patient*. Remember that they all develop at differing rates. Be *forgiving of mistakes and remember they're not yet finished.*

It's easy to overlook that. Especially when your child does something wrong. Actually I don't like to use the word wrong because whatever children do, they do for their own good reasons and that is right in their eyes. The fact that we don't want them to do it doesn't make it wrong. They just have to learn what's appropriate.

Take going to the supermarket for example. Now you know you have a quiet, well-behaved little angel at home – where everything's familiar. But the minute you take your child out she turns into an unmanageable wild animal, interested in exploring everything by handling it, and desperate to experiment with the laws of centrifugal force with the trolley round the aisle corners.

A little story

One of my children was an explorer – very trying and downright terrifying sometimes. She would be so enthralled with exploring she would wander off out of sight, toss herself in the deep end of the swimming pool, climb up things that were high, want to touch things that were hot, etc. We had to be so vigilant. But we also had to have patience. It would have been so easy to constantly think she was 'naughty'. She wasn't naughty; she just was fascinated with her world and as such wanted to learn about it which is a great starting point for education!

Now you may think that your child is doing things like this deliberately just to wind you up whilst other mums' children just seem to follow along obediently.

But another way of looking at it would be that you have an extremely bright child that loves finding out about everything. The supermarket may not be the appropriate place to do that – and they need to understand that. But your child is not 'naughty' for wanting to find things out for themselves.

Be patient. They're learning. They make mistakes. And will go on making different mistakes, at different times all through their lives. But they'll be learning all the time and discoveries and mistakes are a valuable part of their education.

That's another reason why your child needs your investment. The interaction she gets with you and your partner is exactly what she needs to learn. This interaction will be what helps guide her behaviour towards what's acceptable. You don't have to be harsh, bullying or disciplinarian. You just need to have positive interaction. Explain. Talk. Manage your interaction so that your child isn't going to be in situations that spark inappropriate behaviour, think ahead to what will help them learn what is appropriate.

When your child doesn't match up to your expectation of 'good' behaviour it is very easy to get into the habit of reacting to them as though they were 'naughty'. But I don't see children as naughty. I see them as learning and getting it wrong a lot of the time, but that's not a crime. Our job is to guide them to what is appropriate.

Allow them to be the people they are. That doesn't mean to say that they can govern your life and everyone else's. They have to understand that they are part of a large community. And they have to understand that, just the same as everyone else, sometimes they don't get their way, or their wishes met, and they have to learn to accept 'no'.

As long as your child gets the same consideration as everyone else, they soon become accepting. Not getting their own way all the time is an important lesson to learn – none of us do. But, like us, they won't mind that as long as they understand and feel *valued* and *loved*.

The love between you

All this interaction with your child, all the time you spend with them, your attention to them, that's what makes them feel valued and loved. It's not about you never denying your child things. That's inevitable. What's important is your positive, loving input. Children who feel valued and loved nearly always want to please you. And your relationship gets better and better.

I say – nearly always – as there's always one or two strong will powers that you never seem to manage at all, are totally draining, and seem to take ages and ages to get it. And some just go on being extremely challenging with everything you say for the whole of their life. That's just the way they are. They're often the brightest ones.

But mostly children respond to love.

Love makes everyone happy. It makes you happy. It makes your child happy.

Love doesn't have to be soppy. It doesn't have to mean never saying no. But it *does* have to be consistent. It does have to be unconditional. It has to be demonstrated. And never taken for granted.

Sometimes *love is taken for granted.*

Sometimes, because of all the other pressures mums are under, love gets overlooked, buried, or remains unused and unexpressed. Just like in some tired old marriages.

Sometimes we are so busy with the business of doing motherhood things, going through the mechanics of it like laundering babygrows, sterilising stuff, clearing toys, ordering kids about, trying to think up another way to stop them putting the Tablet in the loo when you're not looking, that we *forget to love them*. We forget that the love we feel deep down inside needs openly *expressing*.

We forget to *readily, regularly and unreservedly express our love for them to them.*

I don't mean gush all over them, or slobber all over them, or suffocate them with over-demonstrative gestures. Kids hate that. And I don't mean indulge their every whim or allow abusive behaviour on their part. Neither do I mean never being tough when it's required – the toughest love of all – like; 'no you can't have a chocolate bar,' even though you'd love to give them what they want'. Kids know that allowing them what they want all the time isn't necessarily an expression of love; they just think you're soft. They don't respect you when you always give in to them.

So what do I mean when I say an expression of love?

Of course I mean some physical demonstrations, of course I mean all the cuddles, hugs and kisses you give.

But I mean something else as well.

<u>A little story</u>

My eldest daughter summed it up for me so nicely when I asked her (at ten) what she would have in a mum if she could start from scratch and make one up herself. She didn't actually use the word 'love' but I could feel from her answers that love was totally enmeshed in what she was talking about. She answered very quickly and very simply.

She said; 'someone who cares, someone who listens, and someone you can turn to'.

I have learnt that loving kids isn't only about all those cuddles and kisses which are so very important. It is also about *trust* and *respect*. And I think this is what she was also saying. She was saying that she would want to be able to *trust* that someone cared and loved her, trust that they *respected* her enough to listen and be concerned about what she was saying, and trust that they were *always there for her*. That she could trust the way they *behaved*.

I think that is what our love for our kids is about. Trust and respect and general behaviour as well as the demonstrative stuff. They trust we love them even though they do things wrong, even though we're at war with them sometimes, even though we're all ratty and tired occasionally.

All the kisses and cuddles you can heap upon them will not reassure them that you love them if you are behaving towards them at other times in a way that makes them doubt your love, or which makes them fearful, which makes them lose their respect for you, or in a way which is not a way a person who loves another behaves.

We all have tempers. We all get ratty. We all go over the top and shout and scream sometimes. (Of course we shouldn't be doing that, and never hitting, it's wrong and abusive and if we're resorting to that we perhaps need to seek some support). We all have moods. We all get tired. That's accepted. Kids accept that mums have moods and strops too. And kids respect apologies, by the way. As we would like them to apologise for their own offensive behaviour.

But what I believe shows them that you love them through all this is the fact that despite the occasional blip you generally behave in a consistent, caring and considerate way. You have a moral code of behaviour, show consistent concern for them, *and show respect for who they are, what they say, and what they want to do, and have empathy for their feelings*. It's your consistent way of behaving *towards* them for most of the time that lets kids know you love them, despite losing it occasionally, which we all do.

Kids soon see through the fact that you're giving them slobbery kisses now, or tossing out easy words like 'love you' as you part, to make up for the fact that you *can't be bothered* most of the time. As I said, they're very astute. And bothering *matters* a lot to them.

Bothering with them in that way is an expression of your love for them, but one which can so very often be the first to disappear when mums get over busy with less important tasks like housework for example, or obsessed with less important behaviours like perfection.

<u>A little story</u>

I'd caught myself doing it. I'd caught myself going into whinge overdrive, thinking only about how awful the kids had been (an awful statement in itself if you think about it), how bloody-minded, defiant and difficult they were, how everything was a mess and life's a bitch. Moan. Moan. Moan.

Then, one amazingly enlightening day, when I could see beyond the Vaseline I'd smeared on my nose end (sore from all the sobbing), I thought; hey, just a minute. I'm not happy with this. The kids certainly aren't happy with this. We're all getting on to one another. What on earth am I doing?

So I turned round from getting on at them. I stopped and asked them how they felt. I explained how I was feeling. I showed them lots of concern and care and general Tender Loving Care, I stopped slaving over tidy house and good kids and just had a nice relaxed time with them watching a video and Hey Presto! Everything magically changed. They changed from being little demons into being contented little children. In an instant.

It was amazing. I tried it again and again. It worked every time. Every time things were getting wretched and heated and I felt surrounded by grumpy kids I realised that I'd been too busy with other stuff and not busy enough with the important job of loving my kids. Of behaving in a loving, caring, considerate way towards them. Of simply expressing my heartfelt love for them.

What's the good of love if it's not expressed? What's the good of love if the recipient never *feels* it?

If things between your little ones and you aren't right, stop what you're busy with and love yourselves and them better. Little things matter, in more ways than one. Love is the best thing of all. *Don't forget to express it.*

Express your love by your attention

Love requires attention. Time and attention.

Before you shrivel with fear that I might be suggesting that you don't give enough of your time, before you start thinking that I'm having an underhand dig at mothers who want a career, I'm not.

I'm not suggesting that you need to be with your children one hundred percent of the time. I'm not suggesting you give all your time to them and take none for yourself. Time for you is as essential as time for them. Your fitness of mind and spirit will help you to be the kind of mum they need, and mothering can be all give, give, give. You need to recuperate some of that.

I'm not suggesting kids have to stop your life, although they will change it. I'm not suggesting that you shouldn't have other interests, work, or other pursuits as well.

No mother should be, or needs to be, always and exclusively with her child. It's not healthy. It doesn't necessarily make happy kids. Mums need rest and recuperation and contrast because time with children certainly depletes the batteries.

And neither am I suggesting that you are a servant to them, not telling them off, never saying 'no', or being a slave to their every whim or demand, giving them everything they want. None of that's good for them, good for their welfare or social development, or their understanding of how they fit into a society or how living together works.

I'm talking about spending some time *focussed* on them, however small a chunk of time it is. Attaching importance to spending time with them *on their terms*. Making time for them a priority, even if it is a small moment, it all counts.

Time for just being there. To pay attention to conversations. To pay attention to listening. Being attentive, to the exclusion of other things.

Every one of those attentive times will help to build the relationship between you both that will have the greatest effect. It will affect how they behave, how they respond to you and consequently how you feel. How valued and loved they feel. That's why your attention matters.

Expressing your love by just being there

So what do I mean by just 'being there'?

I do not mean 'Quality Time'. That horrible tag someone's invented to excuse all the times when they're not there, to excuse the times we really don't want to be bothered with our kids – and we all have those.

What's important is to allow opportunities to give the kids attention when the *kids* want it, not when we want to give it, to just *be around*.

So they can dip into cuddles or comfort when they're needed. Time for the simplicity of contact, touching and holding, story on knee. Or simply knowing you're there as 'back up'. It makes them feel safe, even if you're not actually interacting. Just like us taking a friend to a strange party for moral support and not needing to speak to them all evening.

These are some of the most important times for small children, irreplaceable times I wouldn't want to have not been there for, or to hand over to someone else. Time for demonstrating our commitment and love. Absolutely fundamentally simple times that at times drive you bonkers. But I think they mean so much to young children.

A little story

One of the times my daughter always said 'I love you, mummy' was when I was helping her wipe her bottom. It was almost as if that slightly yucky task was one she really appreciated I would rather not do but I did it because I cared. Means a lot to me that!

These are the times that tell kids they matter. That help towards building that special relationship. That builds trust and respect, so that your kids trust you enough to believe what you say, respond to you, want to do what you say, (even if only sometimes), understand that you're for them.

You being there matters to kids and builds bonds.

How your child behaves is influenced by this bond, not as a result of you 'disciplining' them, as if discipline was something separate that you switch on when you take over care of them.

I have a big dislike of this word discipline that parents like to wave about like a big stick as if it was something outside them. Any 'discipline', for want of a better word, you might have, is not a separate thing, it is intertwined with relationship, it is about the understanding between you and your child, and only about that. Understanding. And mutual respect.

A little story

For example, the children in the classes I've taught and I had an 'understanding' between us about behaviour, about our responsibility not to disrupt others, about our responsibility to care. So discipline was never a problem. I was horrified to have a parent come in and advise me to smack her child because, she said, it would be necessary. It just wasn't. I couldn't make her understand that. She never believed that while her child was in school there was never a problem. It was never all perfection in my classroom, far from it; we'd just communicated what was acceptable and what wasn't by just being together a lot.

That kind of communication comes from being there with your child, switched on to them, establishing eye contact and making a commitment to get up (yet again) and move them from doing something wrong, onto doing something right, spending time explaining. All these times are opportunities to moderate behaviour, show what's appropriate, get your child to respond to you, and which all require you to be there.

Being there is the single most important thing you can do.

Think seriously about how much of this precious time to be there, that flies by so quickly, you want to hand over to someone else.

Expressing your love by conversations

Don't endless conversations about why the cat's got a tail, where the poo comes from and how do aeroplanes stay up wear you down?

Definitely! That's why your time away is so important. Because your child *needs* you to *keep on* having these conversations.

Conversations like these between you and your child are not only a valuable learning tool – I'm sure my kids learnt more during that time sitting on the toilet conversing with me while waiting for that satisfying plop than anything – but they are one of the best ways to establish your relationship. Relationships are based on communication. Especially conversation.

Conversations make the kids feel you are interested, that they are important, valued and worthy. Ignoring your kids' thirst for conversation and understanding of things (hence their endless questions) is ignoring a great opportunity to open lines of communication, to develop their intelligence, to develop your relationship. It's an opportunity for you to demonstrate your respect for them and what they say and to value their comments and opinions even if they are a bit weird.

And the best conversations are always those that happen in those impromptu moments. Like the one sitting on the bench outside M & S one day when one of mine suddenly started discussing men wearing underpants. The chap next to us suddenly looked down at his flies and crossed his legs.

Those wonderful conversations that just don't happen if your mind is elsewhere or you're checking emails on your mobile.

<u>A little story</u>

"Daddies have tails, don't they mummy?" said my youngest.

"Mmm. Yes. Sort of." I was a bit distracted. Shame on me!

"And little girls have bottoms."

I started to pay attention! "Do they? Oh! So what do mummies have?"

She thinks a moment.

"Mummies have fur!"

They're brilliant. Essential. So valuable. The kids learn so much just through chat. So will you. About the way your child's mind ticks. Handy for you. Handy for your child because it makes them feel you are on their side.

It doesn't matter what you know or don't know. It doesn't matter what you end up talking about. It doesn't matter what you're doing, you can usually fit a conversation in any place, as long as you're open to it and listening.

Attention to our small children is priceless. As I said, you don't have to be with them all the time, but when you are with them, pay attention to their talk. Stop Tweeting or surfing on your Iphone, commit yourself to them, talk to them, answer their questions, point things out, and listen. Communicate.

It matters more than social networking. More than anything for this period of time.

Expressing your love by listening

Listening increases your chances in the relationship stakes enormously.

Listening is one of the things we are all so bad at. I know adults who are so bad at listening. They regurgitate all their own mundane bits then when it's their turn to listen they go all glazed eyed and start yawning, it's so bloody annoying.

The children need to know you're listening and not secretly thinking about Facebook. Look at them, establish eye contact, make intelligent answers, not 'that's nice dear'. Converse as a result of your listening.

It may only take a minute or two but showing an interest in what they're saying makes them feel so special and important, shows them you respect them enough to listen and makes them feel worthy and that you're committed to them.

If you show them how you listen to them, then it really helps when you want them to listen to you. If listening and responding to each other is part of your relationship, listening and responding to what you ask becomes second nature to them. Make time for listening and responding in your family rather than just ignoring each other while you all stare at a screen.

Listening and responding is a good habit to establish in a family. It will also be invaluable when you ask 'don't jump on grandma's settee'. Or 'don't put your finger in *there*!' Or *'stop!'* when they're about to dash out into the road. Essential when they're teenagers! Listening and responding are important skills to practice for you and for them.

This type of love and attention is the best kind you could give. And best of all it doesn't cost any money. It doesn't cost the price of a trip to McDonalds. It's less than the latest mobile phone. It's free. It's priceless.

It matters so much.

You might not think so. You might think you are getting nowhere. This is the same for all of us. The same for me. The same for all mums. Ask any of your honest friends.

But take courage, stick at it. And you will be rewarded with those little golden moments with your child when everything is as near perfect as it could be.

Love makes them independent

Some people think that too much love poured on a child makes them soft, or clingy, or dependent. It doesn't. Expressing your love to your child does not make them soft. It's the other way round. Love makes them feel secure, gives them confidence. Not being loved makes children feel insecure and lacking in confidence.

Loved, valued and cared for kids are the strong confident ones. It's confidence that enables them to go out into the world and be independent.

You'll have done everything right as a mum, you'll have been a good mum, if you make your kids feel like that.

Children know where love is. They know if it's there. Not by you treating them in Toys R Us or taking them to Disneyland; they know whether you love them by your *day to day contact* with them. By how you live together. How you treat them at home most of the time. When life's ordinary. A blip doesn't matter. Big treats don't matter that much either in the big scheme of things. It's the smallest of small daily habits that matter most because all added up they make a life. They build the biggest part of that warm loving relationship. And, as well as making you all happy, that relationship is what grows their independence.

It starts right now. Right with them being tiny. However big or small they are your relationship with your child is precious. It's precious to them and it's precious *to you*. Don't waste a second with less important stuff. This time doesn't last.

Your child will become independent and go so quickly – despite the fact that you may find that hard to believe right now. Other things can wait – your child will not. It all changes SO quickly.

Being flexible

Change can catch you out. Your child changes so rapidly you just get one phase worked out and they're on to the next one.

You'll have to make an effort to keep up. There is never *one type fits all* method of being a mum. There isn't a method that doesn't have an expiry date. Your child grows and changes every day. So you are going to have to grow and change every day too. Be prepared.

This is where *being* flexible, adaptable, observant and open to new things all the time will help you cope. Mostly by *not expecting* things to stay the same.

Thinking about all the things I've mentioned in the other sections will help towards building this relationship. But it *will* be a fluid one, always developing in new and different ways as your child does. Be prepared for it to be like that.

And while you and your child go through these changes make sure you get in all the holding, touching, tickling, hugging, stroking, carrying, caressing, hand-holding, napping together and physical closeness you can because that all changes too. And your child will probably go through a phase of not hand-holding, not hugging or touching, not even wanting to walk beside you once they hit teens. So don't miss out now. Enjoy it while it's here. It's all helping you both to be close in more ways than just the physical. Although some children don't like physical closeness and you have to go with that too.

A little story

My youngest went through a stage of refusing to be kissed or not kissing anyone when she was little. I felt that quite hard. A year or two later she was the one doing all the kissing and throwing her arms round me all the time. Now she's grown people always remark that she is such an affectionate young adult giving anyone a lovely hug. I'd never have guessed. I forgot; everything always changes!

There will be good times in your relationship. There will be horrendous times. They will all pass. There will be conflict between you some of the time – a lot of the time it may seem. There will be occasions of peacefulness. There'll be confusion and 'why are they doing that?' popping into your head now and then. This is all a normal part of all relationships. Don't worry about it. Just relax. Just keep on loving. Keep thinking. Appreciate the lovely bits.

And remember: any relationship, however special is about give *and take*.

You need to take something for yourself too. You need to *look after yourself*.

Look after yourself too

This is still SO important. The relationship with your child can be beautiful. It is also extremely draining.

Being with the under fives for long periods of time can be exhausting, exasperating and wearing.

You will not be able to maintain a good relationship where you both feel happy when you are used up and have had no time away from it to recharge. So don't forget to think about you too.

Thinking about the 'You' part of this relationship:

- Building a relationship with your child is not about you being the only one doing the giving.
- Expect some give from your child too. Encourage respect from him for your wellbeing as you respect his wellbeing.
- He will not respect your wellbeing if you don't respect it yourself and demonstrate how you do this. I.e. by looking after yourself.
- This might mean him understanding that you are 'off limits' for half an hour while you relax and he occupies himself.
- You will need to take time away from your child. Good relationships are not based on one hundred percent attendance. In fact, that can have the opposite effect.
- Remember to behave towards your child as you would wish him to behave towards you. *Equally*, remember to behave towards *yourself* as you would wish him to behave towards you.
- Relationship building is about *mutual* love, respect, understanding, tolerance, care, consideration, trust, and honesty.
- Love yourself as you love your child.
- Enjoy a realistic relationship. You don't need to be perfect to enjoy! Happiness doesn't come from perfection.

Tip-Bit No 8: Naughtiness and Punishments
Why kids do what they do and how to change it

I want to start by stopping!

I want to start by no longer using those abominable words; naughtiness and punishment.

And I want to stick my neck out and suggest that most *children of nought to five years do not do things that are 'naughty' as some parents think,* and *they do not deserve punishment.*

Rubbish – you're probably thinking – let me explain.

Children make mistakes. Children do things wrong. Children are not finished yet, they are developing and learning all the time. Mistakes are not deliberately being naughty. (Although sometimes they do things deliberately – they still have a reason). Children make mistakes all the time as they try to understand, explore their world and fit into our complex adult way of behaving.

Children learn the way to behave by seeing and feeling how the people around them behave. And I believe that children rarely do things 'wrong' or behave 'badly' (anyway that's our view, not theirs), with particular *intention* to be bad or wrong. They have genuine reasons for doing what they do.

What I believe we have to do is to try and understand those reasons, explain to them why we want them to do things differently, and demonstrate through our own behaviour, as well as telling them, that all of us have to be aware of the *consequences* of our actions.

Basically, we all want our children to have 'good' behaviour. Or, the other way round, we don't want them to behave 'badly'.

We don't want things broken, rooms trashed, people bashed, folks upset, toys snatched, things abused. Obviously we don't.

Why? Not because it's 'naughty' but more importantly because *it affects and upsets others and our environment, (our home being the child's first environment).* That's the point that matters.

Instead, we want behaviour that shows *consideration* for others, their feelings, and their possessions, for the environment, for our morals.

Most things children do wrong are just a misunderstanding of this simple consideration.

And they do it because a) they don't understand yet why they shouldn't – they're not old or mature enough to see beyond their own immediate needs and wants, they don't have the self control. Or b) they are beginning to understand, but are too absorbed in what they are doing and forget to practice it, or decide to take the risk, still being the egocentric little so-and-sos little kids are.

This is a bit over-simplified. But when you look at 'bad' behaviour from this point of view, it helps you to be patient with kids' mistakes. And us mums all need a hell of a lot of patience and tolerance with the endless mistakes small children make if we're going to help them overcome their egocentric passion to do things like finger painting on the kitchen wall, if we're going to tolerate the irritating things they do and help them to see it from another's point of view.

We also perhaps need never to forget that they *are young*. They might just be too tired, too upset, too immature, or just too downright bloody-minded at that particular point in time to achieve what we're asking of them.

And if you're anything like me, you'll need to exercise every last bit of patience you have if you're not going to completely lose it and go blundering blindly into that hateful punishment mode.

I believe, (when I'm all calm and relaxed and open to reason – not often!), that there is actually no need for any such thing as punishment.

I also believe that punishments are doled out to kids not because it achieves anything, but because parents lose sight of humanity, or are pushed beyond the limits of endurance by particular headstrong kids (we've all known them) or other pressures. Or parents are simply eager to get one up on the kids, or satisfy their desire for revenge. (Doesn't revenge make you feel bad afterwards?)

I also completely understand all parents who've got to this point – I have too – we wouldn't be human if we didn't sometimes. We've all lost it now and then. We too make mistakes.

But we perhaps need to understand that this *is* a mistake on *our* part. That punishment is *not* appropriate and not something that should be happening. It is not a mistake we should continue to be making.

So if not punishment, what then? What can we do to move kids away from undesirable behaviour towards doing what's acceptable?

We can use the idea 'cause and effect'.

Even babies understand cause and effect.

Baby cries, mum appears. Baby learns his crying causes the effect of mum's attention, which was what he wanted.

Infant bangs empty beaker on high chair tray. Mum refills beaker.

Toddler throws wobbly in the shop. Mum gives him sweets to keep him quiet.

Children very quickly understand certain behaviours cause certain effects. Therefore you have the most effective tool at your disposal for helping your child to achieve the sort of behaviour you want; using the idea of cause and effect for your own advantage. Or consequence.

You can demonstrate to the child the *consequence* of his behaviour and explain rather than punish from which he learns nothing. (E.g. the consequence of asking politely is more likely to get them what they want – having a tantrum at the checkout doesn't).

Look at it from the point of view of privilege. Our hard work, our devotion to others, has awarded us the consequence and privilege of nice homes, lots of nice possessions, nice people to be with, and nice things for our children.

And we all know that we have to go on behaving in certain ways to create the effect of privileges.

Our children have a great many privileges. Nice homes, nice toys, loving people around them.

If those things are abused then I think it is right to demonstrate that these privileges will not be earned. That behaviour causes a different effect. This is a fundamental lesson they have to learn. A lesson for life.

At the child's simple level, throwing toys, or breaking things has the effect of the child not having those things to use. Violent, aggressive or abusive behaviour towards others has the effect of loved ones not wanting to be around the child for a while, the child perhaps having to be on their own a bit. Rude or demanding behaviour has the effect of the child *not* getting what they want. Polite considerate behaviour has the effect of them getting what they want.

Do you see how, rather than punishment, the child's actions have led to the effect of loss of the privilege different behaviour would gain them?

Punishment is something done *to kids by parents*. Which makes them angry and resentful and hardly ever alters their behaviour for the better.

The loss of a privilege has to be shown as being an effect of the *child's own* behaviour, is something which *the child* is responsible for and *they can equally cause a different effect*. (That's important).

It needs to be explained to them what is happening and why. Also explained what's *desirable* so that they have the chance to get it right, rather than only learning from doing it wrong. We need to consistently remind children that consideration for others and the things around them leads to the privilege of contact with those things. And how the opposite behaviour has the reverse effect.

This idea is fundamental to all our relationships, whoever we are, young or old, yet we sometimes forget it. It's important we practice it though.

We may forgive occasional strops, moods and tantrums, (and we all have those) but continual rudeness or abuse is not acceptable and does not have the effect of loving relationships. Loving relationships are what govern behaviour. Ours included.

Of course, we need to be flexible. We need to take into account age, maturity, emotions at present time, circumstances at present time, and the reason why a child is behaving like she is. But I'm not sure there's a reason or an excuse for what is, as far as I see it, abusive behaviour by some young children of others, their mum included! Children benefit from understanding that *having other loving beings in our life is the very best thing anyone could have*. They need to take care of that and work to cause that effect.

Having this fundamental idea about cause and effect really helps towards managing your child's behaviour. It helped me to explain to my kids the *why*.

Kids deserve reasons for what we ask of them. Our basic fundamental reason is that: although we have empathy for their lack of maturity, their mistakes and their emotions, *our children need to learn to be as considerate towards others and the environment as we are ourselves.*

Which leads us towards looking *at our own behaviour* towards our children. At whether we demonstrate consideration in the way we respond to them.

How do we respond to our children?

Just as we would encourage our children to show consideration for others – adult or otherwise – that is; all human beings, then I believe our behaviour towards our children should also demonstrate consideration for others – *child* or otherwise. We're not, in my view, allowed to shout at or bully or punish them just because they're kids and they're smaller than we are.

How we respond to our kids, I believe, has a big effect on how they continue to behave.

Nagging, shouting and threatening are all ineffective and we all keep on doing it because nagging, shouting and threatening seem to be modes of behaviour that we've been conditioned to believe is what parents do. And admittedly it's sometimes easier. It might be easier but it's not effective in the long term when they switch off to us.

But just like some teachers think that to be a teacher they must shout, some parents seem to believe that to be a parent they must nag, shout and threaten

You don't have to be nagging, shouting and threatening. Not only is it ineffective at getting children to do what you want, it also destroys your good relationship with your child. It has no positive outcomes whatsoever. Doesn't even make you feel good.

So it pays to try harder not to. Use other responses. We need to think more carefully. We need to consider whether we would like to see our *own* behaviour in our children. We need to look carefully at whether our behaviour towards our child is having the desired effect, whether anything's changing, because if it's not then it's not worth carrying on.

For example; ever got the feeling that sometimes when you speak to your kids it's like talking to brick walls?

Definitely!

Got the feeling that what you say falls on deaf ears?

Exactly!

Feel frustrated because you're saying the same things over and over again and it's having no effect?

Absolutely!

Simple answer: then stop it.

So many things our children do irritate us enormously. But that's all they are; irritating. We don't always have to nag them to stop it. So much of what they do isn't important. So I think it works better to ignore those things, *say nothing* and save our voice for the big things. Continually going on about the little things they do makes kids totally switch off. And it has no effect.

There are millions of irritating little things our kids do all the time, just because those are the things kids do. But sometimes these things become so magnified in our minds we overlook the harmlessness of them, and forget all the nice things about our children. Maybe if you can only see the bad things right now, perhaps you could try and remember that it is not because your child is 'bad'. It's just that they're irritating to *you* – that's *your* problem not theirs. And if you're constantly irritated by them, you need time off, time away, to help you see it from a refreshed point of view.

And there are so many wonderfully good things about our beautiful children we must try not to nag them all the time about their irritating side.

Would you like to listen to a tape of yourself nagging all day long? Me neither! But that thought taught me to look at what I say, at how much of what I say has *no tangible effect*. And that I perhaps should limit my requests to the things I *am* going to carry through, the important things, or explain. And definitely not toss out constant threats that I haven't a hope of carrying out, (or any intention come to that).

A little story

Many is the time friends and I have regretted making threats because

a) you have to carry them out, even though you don't want to, for your kids to take any notice, and

b) if you don't carry them out kids believe they don't have to worry/listen to/take seriously what mum says.

Many is the time in desperate moments I've been about to threaten; 'if you don't put your toys away then there'll be no gaming tonight' then I stop and think; idiot! I know kids don't put toys away. I know it's a great relief to have them use the computer sometimes. I know it's going to be agony to carry this threat out. So instead I'd say it from a more positive perspective 'if you put your toys away now we can have tea then you can go on your game' so they can see a consequence of complying with my request.

What we say needs to be *honest. It needs to demonstrate a way of behaving we would be happy to see in them.* Offer them a positive consequence of doing what we ask rather than shouting at them. And while we're on that subject would we be happy with our child shouting at us? Then should we be shouting at them?

A little story

I once went in for a day's teaching with no voice. I thought to myself; 'how am I going to make the kids hear me (thirty-six of them) with no voice? How am I going to make myself heard over all the noise?'

It was the quietest day I've ever had and I learnt a valuable lesson that day: the quieter you are with kids the quieter they will be in return. I don't have to be loud or shout to make myself heard. Also true now I'm a parent.

Shouting is a bit like punishment; we resort to it when we're losing our self-control. (Yep; me too on occasions!) It's not something we ought to be doing. I hate myself afterwards. We don't like it when folks shout at us.

How does your child speak to you?

How do you speak to your child?

You might surprise yourself if you investigated, or tried something different.

And a final tip I'd like to offer is about 'answering back'. I.e. *you* answering back, not the child.

Never argue with your child. They always win. They have an answer for everything, or throw a wobbly, and how can you argue a point with someone who has absolutely no sense of reason at this stage? And they can't answer you back if you haven't said anything.

I have a far better strategy taught to me by another mum. That is to say nothing. You have your say, you give your reasons, tell them it's not going to change however much they argue, then you plop your lips together and *remain silent*.

It stops you becoming frustrated with the heat of fruitless argument. It stops your child from arguing because if there's no one saying anything then there's no argument. You may even walk away. It's great for defusing an impending fight sometimes. Doesn't always work, but when it does it's really worth it. See if it works for you. You'll have to grit your teeth to stop yourself but it's better than shouting, threatening or nagging.

All said and done what we want is an easy life and nice children.

Sometimes it all seems too much hard work, especially if you are doing most of it on your own, or are with your children for long periods of time. I can appreciate this. I've felt it too.

But care of your relationship is worth it. Care with the way you treat your child. Looking at your child's reasons for doing what they do and looking at your own responses to their behaviour will give you a much better chance of a good relationship, and good kids. Cause and effect works for you too.

Sometimes it may be that we are unintentionally causing bad behaviour in our kids by making the effect of their behaviour worthwhile. Eg. Mum buys kid sweets to keep him quiet when he throws a wobbly in the sweet shop. The kid sees the effect of his bad behaviour is sweets. If mum did this the other way round, told the child beforehand that she is going into the shop and if he behaves well he will get a treat when they get home, then the kid sees his good behaviour causes the effect of being given the treat. You have to be tough about the sweets if he doesn't manage it; he definitely will next time, you'll see.

I am realistic. It doesn't always work as sweetly as this. But you can see where I'm heading. And we have to start small and pick things the kid *can* achieve to encourage them to succeed rather than fail and be punished.

It's hard work controlling yourself sometimes. But hard work at the beginning makes an easier life later on. Bad habits (yours and the child's) are harder to crack than good habits are to establish. Be consistent.

Think about cause and effect. In both of you. It might help to make your relationship with your child better, and that's the best thing for mums.

A good relationship makes for happy people. Happy mums and happy kids. That's what really matters.

Chapter Nine

Ongrowing

On-growing through mumhood is a life's journey – you are of course a mum for life.

But it's an amazing wondrous journey which you are only really at the start of when you first give birth. As you journey through it, the experiences you encounter along the way will transform and enlighten you, teach and develop many skills and talents you never even knew you were capable of. Your sense of responsibility and care, commitment and respect will probably double, treble even. You grow and mature in ways that are inconceivable.

I can quite shock myself when I think how irresponsible and disrespectful I might have been pre-mumhood. But we learn as we go.

The journey will sometimes be full of storms and tornadoes, take you through choppy seas and uncharted territories, big tides and rapids, with inevitably the odd iceberg. It will also have many times of sweet plain sailing, when the current of life will carry you along smoothly, the going is steady and your sails are gently filled with the easy breeze of a good life and happiness.

That's what you want to aim for. Even though you can't always predict the parenting weather.

Growing as a person, learning and changing, being happy or sad, is all part of anyone's journey, parent or not. Your life as a parent, and as a *person*, needs within it the same elements as anyone else's, parent or not, in order for it to be enjoyable.

The pitfall for many women is that, as soon as they become mothers, they forget this simple fact. Forget to pay attention to other elements especially if they're giving up the work they did before as they devote themselves to their mumhood, their new baby, or are busy with a whirlwind toddler or a challenging pre-schooler.

Having a new baby in the house is such a celebratory, joyous time. Like having a birthday every day of the week. You just want to attend to this miraculous being that's now in your life and forego everything else. And that's great. It feels great – it's good to do.

But sometimes you can get so absorbed in doing that, so attentive to the needs of your child, even years on, that you can forget that you need attention too, completely forget your own needs. And it gets even more complicated when those needs have changed while your back was turned and you're not sure what you need any more. What you want to do. Or even what makes you feel good now.

Recognising what's happening

My needs changed dramatically and regularly during those first few years that my babies grew. *I* changed dramatically, although it took a while for me to recognise what was happening to me. Especially since I was *so* absorbed by my beautiful baby.

Being a mum can be an all-consuming, overwhelming life's work. It is certainly a life's commitment. It will take up enormous amounts of time and energy.

But not *all* of it – it is important that it doesn't.

As you can think about and choose your role and your work as a parent, you can also choose to bring other elements into your life besides your mum tasks. And how happy you are while you are a mum is very much dependent on these choices.

Being happy is a choice - so I've read. I have often thought I bet it wasn't a mother who wrote it! It certainly feels as if the circumstances and commitments you have as a parent take away your choice.

I have also read that people succumb to depression because they feel that their world, as they know it, is falling apart. That the meaning they attached to their world has completely altered. When I read that I felt as if they were *exactly* talking about mums. Because that is exactly what happens to you when you become a mum. Your world, as it was before, falls apart. That's not necessarily in a bad way. But *everything changes*.

It's bound to. It has to really. To maintain that it doesn't, or fight for it not to, is to deny an opportunity for your own personal development, learning and growth.

But handling those changes, and the choices you make as a consequence of them, will also influence how happy you feel with what you're doing. And to handle them you have to actually understand them and accept that they are happening to you in the first place.

The reality is that *all* experiences change us. However big or small those experiences are. Whether they are as traumatic as moving house, having someone die, breaking off a partnership, changing jobs, or as seemingly small and insignificant as going to the theatre, reading the work of an author you haven't come across before, buying a new style, networking with someone new online.

These new experiences *all* will have an impact, even if you're not aware of it at the time. So acknowledge that this is true.

However, even knowing this, most of us are completely *unprepared* for the dynamic change and impact that having a baby makes to us. To us personally, and to our lives.

Changing

Becoming a mother *does* change us enormously. This may not be apparent at first. You may not want to accept that at all – ever. But there's no getting away from the stark, staggering truth; having a baby changes a girl.

And with change there are two things you have to face.

The first: *you are losing some of what you once were*.

The second: *you are growing into someone new*.

And these are two big issues you need to come to terms with and handle if you want to be happy. If you want to keep happy even though you are going through the falling apart of your world as you knew it. If you want to continue to be the best mum you can be it matters that you acknowledge this and learn how to adapt to a new and different contentment.

It is well recognised that there are two huge transitions in a woman's life; puberty and menopause. I would say there's another huge transition in between those two; the transition that takes place as a woman becomes a mother.

Just like with puberty and menopause this transition takes time, it's very emotive, very unsettling, and yet you have to get on with living and coping and managing life as if it wasn't. But unlike puberty and menopause, which are expected and accepted – in society too, you are pretty unprepared for this particular personal transition into mumhood. And you've also got another draw on your reserves – your lovely child.

Many of us find it really hard to adapt to change. We cling to old ways like a drowning man clinging to a log. Many parents do this subconsciously making it even harder to adapt to the changes having children inevitably bring.

For women it is particularly hard because it is *their* world on which it has the greatest impact. It is women who make the greatest personal sacrifices. It is your life's plan that suffers the biggest disruption.

However fighting change is futile. To handle it you need to give yourself plenty of understanding and sympathy. Understand that these changes are going to affect you emotionally. Accept it's going to take some adapting to and go with the flow, because you *will* need to adapt.

The great thing about change is that it is about *growing*. Change is a positive, life enhancing progress. It's not just the children who are doing the growing – it's you too. Just because you've reached adulthood doesn't mean to say you've stopped growing or learning or changing. You, like with your child, are never finished. As you nurture the growth of your child, appreciate the same is happening to you.

Trying to stay the same is unhealthy. You will stagnate. You will become dull and down and frustrated. However much you try to 'go back' it will not feel the same as it did before and those feelings can be horrible. It's not good for you or for the people around you. Or for your child. Maintaining that you, and life, are the same as before you had a child also disrespects the duty you have now as a parent who is responsible for the growth and wellbeing of another living being.

How could that not change you?

Instead of trying to keep everything the same as it was before allow yourself to swim with the changes. Allow yourself to grow. Look after yourself as you weather these changes. Go with your feelings and your intuition. Do what you want. Accept yourself as you are now. Be brave about forging ahead into unknown territory, even if it is something or some way of being you'd never normally associate with *you*. Liberate yourself from old expectations.

The exciting thing is you never know what you might discover, but do allow yourself to learn and discover. It's totally uplifting.

Your needs

Having a child, making the transition to being a mum, usually means sacrifice. You gain enormously, but you sacrifice too.

In fact, you make a huge amount of sacrifices when you become a mum. That's inevitable. It's also tough – especially if you were unprepared and I don't think there is anything that could prepare you unless you've been closely involved with others who've become mums before you. Even so, you are different.

It's quite tough to endure the sacrifice of your time, your energy, your personal needs, your previous relationships, your previous confidence, your independence, and a spontaneity about life. All that can disappear.

Personal needs are the greatest sacrifice. That's an area that seems to readily go and which mums tend to forget to pay attention to. It takes a while to handle it.

Some mums become so engrossed in the needs of their child they completely forget to pay attention to their own wants and desires. And some to such an extent they even forget *what those needs are*.

That's why I've kept on repeating throughout this book; 'look after yourself'.

Staying in touch with yourself as a mum now is so important. It is your personal needs and wants not being attended to that can easily steal away that happy feeling. And now I'm not only talking about your needs for a rest or sleep or good food. Those needs usually make themselves known quite readily. I'm talking about your other needs, the less apparent ones, that make you fulfilled as a *person* not only a *mother*.

These might include your need for adult company. Your need to go to the gym, or a walk, or a swim, or a dance. Your need to do some other activity besides mother your child, that is *personal to you*. Your need to have time for other work. Your need to meet adult friends. Your need to have some time alone. Your need to have time for a personal pursuit, creative activity, a course or a class. And lastly to recognise that your tastes will have changed and you will have a need to do *new* things.

These needs are just as important as your need to rest. They must be met too. They are as much of a priority as anyone else's. For you to grow as a person these things need addressing. You must *never* completely sacrifice all your needs to those of your children or wider family. If you don't respect your needs no one else will. Your development is just as important.

Sacrificing all of yourself up to the needs of others doesn't make you a good mum either. It's not good for your child. It isn't good parenting.

Sometimes though, that's how mums make their life fulfilling. I have seen mums who try to satisfy their need for happiness through their children's lives. By making their *whole* life an attendance to their children. They follow the doctrine that if they make their children happy then they are happy.

Now we are all happy if our kids are happy – we all want our children to be happy. Of course we do. But our *own* happiness is our *own responsibility too*; it falls to us to make our own lives happy *outside* of our children as well as through them. Placing all our capacity for our happiness at their door is putting an awful lot of pressure on them. It will soon burden them.

Your happiness is something *you're* in charge of independent of your child's happiness. And finding it will come from attending to *your* personal needs too. Not only those of your child.

Your life as a parent and another person too

A little story

My mum friends and I now recognise how our personal needs have changed gradually over our years of being a mum, as we have changed in ourselves and grown up a bit more. Although we didn't believe at the start that becoming a mum changed us. Neither did we understand, when we did acknowledge it, in what way.

We have changed and grown dramatically. We've talked about it much and we decided that the idea that we might not have changed in all these years of parenting would be a pretty repulsive thought. Because that would mean we hadn't learnt anything. You have to change in order to learn, you have to let go of old ideas in order to embrace new ones.

Through all that time there has been much about being a mum I absolutely loved (being with my gorgeous children) and other things about being a mum I loathed (definitely the domestic side of it). But my mum friends and I found that there were certain less obvious needs that required fulfilling in order for us to feel whole, happy, balanced, and satisfied with our life and work and role as a mother and another person too. It's these we wanted to share.

Some of these less obvious needs lay in having: -

- a balance between everything
- personal pursuits
- contrast
- exercise
- solitude
- stimulation
- recreation
- personal time, without the children sometimes
- love
- choices, instead of staying stuck in an old habit

When we felt unhappy with life it was often because one or some of these needs weren't being met. They'd got shifted down the list of priorities. It didn't seem to matter that our attention to them was only quite small sometimes while other things took over, as long as they got back in balance in the end we felt better.

To keep them in balance you need to be aware of them in the first place. So, to make sure you're fully aware of these less obvious needs, let me show you what they mean in a little more depth.

A balance between everything

Being a mother is a massive balancing act. It's hard enough to achieve all the things a child requires of you without introducing anything else into the equation.

But paying too much attention to one area and not enough to others will soon make you feel off balance.

Balancing your child's needs with your own – even the less immediate ones – is essential to your wellbeing. And your wellbeing matters to your parenting.

It is often the less obvious needs that go the most easily. When you are desperate for food you eventually eat. But sometimes you may feel desperate but for other reasons, like the need for some time away, and it is equally important that you achieve that as soon as you can. Desperation or unhappiness can often be the result of you not paying attention to those less obvious needs, like doing something other than mother your child sometimes.

Children are excellent at employing strategies to defraud you from having some time to yourself and pay attention to your needs. Have you noticed; the minute you get settled with a cuppa, or on the phone, they want something or their attention seeking ploys get louder.

You'll have to be *firm* as well as kind. It matters that you prioritise your children but it also matters that prioritise you too at times because it teaches your child that all people matter not just them. They need to understand this because eventually it makes them nicer people to be with which makes a nicer life for them because people like them, so they have more friends...it's a whole cycle.

So, find ways of balancing, or dovetailing which perhaps describes it better as all can be fitted together sometimes, all the things you want in your life – find a way of dovetailing your needs with your child's. Work and play. Activity and rest. Jobs and love. Kids and adults.

Personal pursuits

To do something other than mother your child just sometimes seems like hard work. A lot of mums I talked to have let go all their personal pursuits once they had a child, and some their work too, so they have very little that they do other than be a mum. That's when they lost touch with their own needs and wants and even their identity.

Being a mum is a wonderful, valuable, worthwhile occupation. But you do need something else to do other than tending your child and its accessories. It's just the same with any workaholic. Being a complete workaholic is not good for you. Being a mumaholic isn't either.

Some women find this fulfilment in activities outside the home. Some women find it in work. Some find it in hobbies, creativity or a mini business at home. Whatever you do, it is so important to introduce other activities into your life that are purely just for you. A weekly swim, get together with friends, grow things, make things, cook, do a class or new activity, book club, whatever.

Very few people feel complete, fulfilled and well when they only have one aspect to their lives. We all need the contrast of varied activities.

Contrast

The need for contrast is often overlooked. However much we love doing something, however much we were good at it, if that was the only thing we did we'd soon feel stale and dissatisfied. 'A change is as good as a rest' the saying goes. Take change to mean contrast and you'll get the same result. But this contrast means introducing something completely opposite to what you'd normally do.

So try and introduce elements, pursuits and activities into your life that are a contrast to what you normally do. E.g. if you normally work at home, you will need to make sure you get out often. If you normally dress casually, dress up for a change. If you have a busy scheduled, time-tabled life, introduce occasions when you just drift and go with the flow. If you rush around most of the time, have times when you slow down. If your work involves masses of people, introduce times of solitude. If you're a normally sedentary person take up an active hobby. Keep it fresh. Keep plenty of contrast in what you do.

Exercise

Don't worry – I don't mean you to suffer!

I know exercise is a dirty word to some. Exercise often means things some people hate. Like hard slog, aching muscles, feelings of inadequacy, competition, gruelling torture, embarrassment, expensive gyms, body-clinging clothing, pain.

I hate all those things too – yet I love my quiet but invigorating walks or bike rides. That's what I do for exercise.

Some people manage to convince themselves that exercise is not for them but we all need some form of exercise for our wellbeing – physical and mental.

It doesn't have to be anything like most people think it has to be and it doesn't have to involve any of the miseries mentioned above. Exercise is just *an opportunity for feeling good.*

Why would you not want that? It's worth a bit of effort to get that surely?

Exercise is just a way of looking after yourself. It is personal to you. It doesn't have to concern anyone else. It doesn't have to have anything to do with your weight or your figure or what you wear. It can be purely for your wellbeing. It's nobody else's business. But you can seek company if you want as that helps with motivation sometimes. Or you can do it on your own and enjoy the opportunity for a good think.

But exercise should be something that you essentially do for *yourself*, to please yourself, to look after yourself, and to feel good about. Because it will make you feel good. It releases chemicals in your brain that induce happiness. Exercise is something all mums definitely need. Exercise is another way of nurturing yourself.

You can get it simply by putting your child in a buggy and going for a brisk walk. This is free, it doesn't matter where you are, it doesn't matter when you do it – it's just so easy. No cost, no outlay, nothing special required. That's all you need to do. A brisk twenty minute walk, several times a week will do. You can walk instead of taking transport or car. You can walk anywhere and everywhere. You just need to get into the habit. That's all. Simple. Just do it. Integrate it into your life so that it becomes as natural a part of your daily rituals as cleaning your teeth.

Or you can swim, cycle, horse ride, jog, dance, box, do a class or group, anything, with or without company, with or without your child, whatever suits. Just do it. Just do what fits in with you best. The benefits are enormous.

You *do* have a need for exercise, however much you try and deny it – for your wellbeing. Don't overlook that important need. Face up to it. You'll soon feel your spirits lift as you whisk along.

Solitude

You also have a need for solitude occasionally, even though you may not be aware of it.

Human beings are very social animals. Our whole culture is geared to being in contact with others. We're so sucked into social networking it becomes an addiction. We're always 'on call' to our mobiles and social media centres.

Culture tries to convince us that being on your own is sad. It's not encouraged and anyone who spends a lot of time on their own is often thought of as peculiar. It's even making people afraid or embarrassed by being on their own.

This attitude needs to change because it's totally inaccurate and very manipulative. We all do need to be on our own sometimes.

Why?

Because being on your own gives you the opportunity to think. To be deeply self-aware. To get in contact with the real you that is inside when all the other influences are gone. To just be your beautiful self. To have a few meditative moments maybe just enjoying the outdoors or some music can be incredibly calming. Mums need those moments.

Being a mum rarely gives you opportunity to be on your own. So it brings contrast to what you normally do. Being on your own might be something you do when you exercise, or follow your own pursuit or hobby, or shop even although you're never strictly on your own in shops.

Being on your own gives you personal space. And everyone needs that. Small moments of solitude can bring you enormous benefits. Lone moments can be beautiful. And can also make the company you normally keep much more attractive.

Stimulation

We all have a need for stimulation too.

Some of the work we do every day is extremely tedious. In fact all work can be tedious at times. Tedium soon leads to boredom and being bored can make you feel dissatisfied and unhappy.

Stimulation doesn't have to mean work or taking an OU degree.

You can get stimulation from conversation, reading, new projects and activities, creating something, going to new places, a challenge, new online groups, even from the telly or surfing the Net if you happen to be looking at the right programme or surfing in the right place. But even the telly and the Net get boring if you do it too much.

Stimulation will often come with contrast. It's usually a change from the norm and something you're not already familiar with. Something that takes you out of your comfort zone will be stimulating.

Keep an eye on your need for stimulation and make sure you're getting enough.

Recreation

Recreation might be an opportunity to take up a stimulating activity, although it doesn't have to be stimulating. Or it could be your opportunity to exercise, or an opportunity for a personal pursuit. Or just chilling out.

But it does have to be is something recreational for *you*, that is for you and you alone, with no other conditions attached. It's often hard to fit in the time for recreation. But it is another essential need that requires your attention.

Recreation is about you creating an opportunity to do something exclusively to you, that engages your attention, but makes you feel *relaxed*. Something that you enjoy, that makes you feel entirely good, and you do it for no other reason than that. Like a bath, a read, a walk, a good film with a friend, lunch out. Whatever. Recreation is all about you having a relaxing enjoyable time whatever form it takes.

Recreation is enjoyment. You have a need for pure enjoyment. See that need gets met.

Personal time without the children

Another major need. But essential. However much you love your children and being with them you still need to be without them sometimes. You also sometimes need exclusive adult company when there are no little ones around.

This isn't about disrespecting the children or loving them any less, it's just about having change, contrast, recharging. We all need time without our loved ones. For example, I love my husband to bits but if I was with him all the time we'd both go mad. We both agree we have needs that are met by others sometimes and we don't respect each other any less because of that. It's the same for being without our gorgeous children sometimes.

You may be able to tie this in with your personal pursuit, or exercise, or solitude or recreation. Whatever; you need to get it in somewhere. Regularly. Don't miss out on fulfilling this need.

Love

You need to remember to keep in touch with love. In the daily 'busyness' of being a parent and working and living a life as a family the need for love can get overlooked. Love requires attention. Love can become so buried – most particularly the *love between the parents*. Everyone finds this bit hard. Because one of the things that changes dramatically when you become parents is the dynamics between you.

You had exclusive time for each other before your child was born. That's gone. There's always someone between you these days it seems – even in the bed. This needs handling. You will need to find a new way of addressing both your needs for loving moments towards each other.

Becoming new parents is stressful. Love doesn't easily get expressed when you're stressed. It will be something you both need to talk about and manage. You will need to explain to your partner how difficult it all is at the moment. And let him say how difficult it is for him too.

Just as I've said you need to stop doing all the non-essential domestic stuff and pay attention to your child, you also need to stop in order to pay attention to each other too. Make time for your relationship. Make time to receive and give love to each other. Take care of your need for love. Your need to maintain a loving relationship between the two of you as well as between you and your child.

Choices

One issue that has a big impact on your life as a mum is *choice*. All through these chapters I've encouraged you to think about the situation you are in and decide what you want to do with it.

I've encouraged you to choose.

When I've heard depressed and dissatisfied and unhappy mums talking about their circumstances, their hardships, and the tough job of a parent, they are nearly always talking about feeling a *victim* of their circumstances.

And sadly, very often they are.

Very often they are at the mercy of their feelings, their enormous workload, their partner's lack of understanding and support, their manipulative children, their poor health, their lack of income, the tough job of being a parent, their job, and the sacrifice of the person they want to be.

Despite modern technology and labour saving devices and convenience foods, despite a so-called modern re-vamp of motherhood, despite equality, and despite our so-called sophisticated, advanced culture and standard of living there are still mums who suffer dreadfully. They suffer dreadful devaluation of their role and work by the people close to them, dreadful conflict between the inherent demands of caring, nurturing, overwhelming commitment to others and the prioritising of their personal self.

Nothing makes you feel worse than being a victim. And quite often women who are mothers are in a situation where they can soon become victims.

Everyone has the chance to make choices, even if hard or tiny. We cannot control all of the things all of the time. We cannot even control everything a bit of the time. But we can control some things, however small, some of the time.

Making choices, however small they seem to be, makes a difference to how you feel. Making a choice to make your needs a priority as much as you can will make a difference. Thinking about the choices talked about in this book will make a difference. Making a choice to change things however small and gradually will make a difference.

To make a difference to how you are feeling you will need to remember to continually look for the opportunity for choice. To reassess as things change and continually make them.

Not forgetting that *happiness is a choice* too.

Thinking about your needs:

- Don't forget them.
- Check the list above regularly.
- Make them a priority too.

Having it all

Women have been accused of wanting it all. They've been accused of wanting a career and wanting children and wanting equality and wanting men to hold the doors open for them too.

I think those doing the accusing have missed the point. And having a career and having children *isn't* 'having it all'. Neither is it having a ball as the term implies.

What women want is the opportunity to do what they want; in the workplace and in the home. Just like men have the opportunity to do what they want.

Women just want what men have; purposeful work, pleasant homes and to raise a family in whatever way suits their personal circumstances. And the *respect* that men have for doing so.

They want the opportunity to work if they desire. The opportunity to devote lots of time to their child if they desire. The opportunity to have their needs as a *person and a mum respected*. The opportunity to fully express their innate abilities to mother their child without being thought of as weak, a liability, a cumbersome dependant or a business risk.

What women want is the *same valued identity* as men have.

What women want is the whole importance of family responsibilities respected as much as business responsibilities are respected. What women want is the opportunity to have the opportunities that men have, and not to be *devalued* by anyone because of their choices. What women want is to be respected for their commitment to their important work of being a mother and raising another member of the human race who will make a valid contribution.

This is, I think, what women really want. Although they seem to be criticised for wanting it, in a way that men are not.

Men are not criticised for doing full-time work when there's children in the house and both partners work. Neither are they criticised for being a 'house dad' whilst their partner earns, they are respected for doing something monumental. Do women get the same respect if they make those choices? NO – it's taken for granted. What women want is that same respect for their choices that men are awarded.

As I said; *women just want the same respect as men enjoy for the same choices* they make through their commitment to work, family and home.

The term 'having it all' is totally disrespectful. It devalues the role of women in raising their families and keeping food on the table in whatever form they decide to do it in their family unit. When do you ever hear the remark 'wanting it all' said about men and the choices they make? Never!

You as a mum deserve the same respect as men get for making similar choices and it is nothing to do with 'having it all' or not. It's about your right to choice. So you *choose*.

Misguided choices

To create a solid family unit takes time and devotion and hard work. Time and devotion will be required for it to be a happy family unit.

Raising a new young family can be such a happy time and to make it so it's important parents are happy with the choices they make.

Happiness can make as huge an impact on the world as big business. Robert Louis Stevenson was right when he said 'There is no duty we so much underrate as the duty of being happy. By being happy we sow anonymous benefits upon the world'.

Some of the choices women make can be misguided. Some of the things women choose to do are sadly not for want of happiness, are not in order to be a better parent, raise a happy family unit or are not even about income, they are to do with other things.

They are to do with things forced on them by a need to be *noticed and valued* and have the respect that working men have, maybe through a working identity that is familiar, through a respected label like 'career' or through the respect of an income.

Women are sometimes trapped by a feeling of need to provide a high income because of the feeling of worth and value it brings when mothering does not. This all pervading work/money ethic – the feeling that every minute must be filled with paid 'work' for a woman to get any kind of credit- does mums no favours. They are hardly even noticed when they're non-earning mums, so they sometimes make other choices they would rather not.

This is the kind of pressure that governs some mums' choices.

But there are only a few good authentic reasons for choosing what you need to do:

- it makes you happy

- it values your kids
- it's what you think is right for you and your kids
- it makes your family work well

Those are the reasons you want to be influencing your choices. Not mass culture pressure. The choices we make affect the choices women in the future make and will eventually change poor attitudes to mothering our kids. We can help increase respect for mums by our authentic choices.

Happiness as a choice

It seems daft to say happiness is a choice. How can we choose what happens to us? Isn't that up to fate? Some people believe not. Some people believe we choose everything in our lives even if subconsciously. Although I have a bit of difficulty believing that entirely.

But what I do believe, what I know to be true, is that we can choose certain things that will influence our happiness.

We can choose to do activities that influence it. We can choose to keep as many positive thoughts in our minds as we can. We can choose to walk about with a smile on our faces instead of a scowl. We can choose to be soft and loving with our kids rather than hard and dictatorial and businesslike. We can choose our reactions to circumstances – choose to break with former patterns of behaviour if they're destructive. It takes practice, but it can be done.

We can choose to slow down and do something about our stress. We can choose a lifestyle we've thought out for ourselves not one everyone else reckons we should choose. We can choose to love our kids for what they are rather than disapprove of their immature skills. We can choose to communicate with them rather than disconnect with them. We can choose how much time we give to work, to our kids, to ourselves. We can choose to pay attention to our needs as a person as well as our duty as a mother.

Those are some ways to choose happiness.

We can choose to commit to it. And by doing so we can demonstrate to other members of society how to commit to it too; family, friends, employers, politicians, schools and all institutions and businesses. Maybe this would change some attitudes.

This is what you can choose, even if you can't choose for your kids not to be here right now because you're a bit stressed and wound up. And if you are feeling that you wish your kids weren't here right now just think the next time you're in the supermarket and your child is bawling their head off – there might be some childless woman looking at you and giving anything to be the mother of your child. And next time you walk through the shopping centre with a restless two-year-old trying to dislocate your arm, there are some women who long to have a little hand to hold theirs. Choose to be happy with what you've got – there may be others who'd long to be in your shoes.

Happiness is *not* a soft option – it is tough sometimes. Tough to uphold convictions, be firm when you want to give your kids what they want yet it would be best not to, make choices even if they're difficult. Just as motherhood is not a soft option simply because we're at home. It is demanding, tough and requires huge strengths. Choices can be tough.

But happiness is always a good criterion to govern your choices. And everything always changes and other choices need making in order to keep a happy equilibrium.

Your children grow up so quickly. Each phase is really quite small in the larger pattern of a life, even though it seems all consuming right now. Everything will end. Your children will grow and leave home.

But you will be a mother forever. You as a person will go on forever. To survive and enjoy motherhood you want to be happy. You need to make choices that you'll be happy with – not ones that keep others happy.

You, as a mother and a woman, are powerful, strong, important, capable, intelligent, devoted, respected and hard working. You have enormous inner strength. There is true courage in getting up and seeing to your child, however you are feeling, day after day for the rest of your life. That's what you do.

You quite rightly deserve to be as happy as you can whilst doing it.

Keep your options for happiness always open, keep it as a governing part of your choices, and you will always find them. And if you can't find them make them.

You're a mum; you are paramount, your contribution as a mother has enormous worth. Choose to be a happy mum too and make your contribution even greater and even more enjoyable. You are one of a community of the most valuable and important working women in the world. You are on a journey. It takes practice and time and choice. Happiness does too.

Following are some things you might like to think of practising on your way. Try picking one or two of these choices occasionally and make mumhood one of the best things you've ever done so far.

Thinking about happiness:

- Practise looking after yourself.
- Practise time away.
- Practise patience, flexibility, adaptability, going with the flow.
- Practise leaving the baby/child in someone else's care sometimes.
- Practise talking to your partner about being a mum and listening to him talking about being a dad – update regularly.
- Practise doing something else in your child's company, explaining to them first.
- Practise talking to your partner about workloads and things that are bugging you.
- Practise doing something different to parenting.
- Practise thinking about other employment if you want it.
- Practise thinking about giving up employment to be with your child if you want to.
- Practise doing some simple rhythmic exercise four times a week.
- Practise being calm.
- Practise acceptance – especially of the fact that you can never seem to get anything finished in one go.
- Practise saying 'no' calmly to your child's demands sometimes.
- Practise spending time with your partner when the kids are not allowed to interrupt.
- Practise thinking about yourself and what *you* really want to do. How are you going to achieve it?
- Practise being *really* honest. Keeping your motives honest to you.
- Practise self-awareness – be aware of how you're behaving, of expectations, of your own needs as well as your child's.
- Practise making your own mind up and keeping 'should' out of your thinking.
- Practise letting go of some of the stuff that stands between you and enjoyment of your children.
- Practise making choices.

- Practise telling yourself that you do a magnificent job, that you are enormously worthy and valuable.
- Practise respect; for yourself, for your child, for your partner, for the work you do and consequently for all mums.
- Practise the loving bits.
- Practise joy. Practice smiling. Practice being happy.

Tip-Bit No 9: How You Influence Your Child's Education

Education is probably the last thing on your mind right now. I bet you can hardly imagine being at that stage.

But what many parents don't understand is that, whatever age your children are, however small or big, their education and their achievement are wholly influenced *by you*. Their education i.e. their learning, starts a long, long time before school and you are the one who affects it. Both now and in the future.

But don't worry, it's not complicated. And it's not academic learning I'm talking about, or is of the only importance.

Children need to learn something more important than academics. They need to learn about *their world* and how to fit into it. How to relate to it and to others. How to operate it and how to cope with it. As well as all the skills they need just to grow and get to grips with living on a daily basis.

Whatever age children are they're learning all the time. And you will be teaching them without even noticing.

You'll be teaching them skills like; using their utensils to eat their dinner. Or even getting finger food in their mouth before that. You'll be encouraging them in the beginnings of speech and the names of things. You will be teaching them how to use the potty or toilet or recognise when they want a wee. You'll be teaching them how to put their clothes on. Or how to build with toys, put toys in the cupboard, or use the computer.

Just take note throughout your day together and you'll realise how much you are already teaching your children. It happens just by interacting together, showing them things, getting them to mimic sounds, encouraging them to walk, demonstrating things by example, talking about the things you see and answering their 'why' questions.

Through all this your children are learning. Through *you* - teachers aren't required here – this kind of learning is equally valuable learning. It is the beginning of their understanding, the basis of all development and learning to come.

That's how you influence your child's education right from the start.

The things you do together at home, *the attention you pay them*, the conversations you have, are the groundwork for everything that follows. The way you engage with them, stimulate them, love them, all the things I've mentioned in the 'Mother and Child' chapter all influence the way in which your child learns and all the learning that will come after. The first three years of a child's life are now recognised to be the kingpin for all that follows. And the learning they do from birth to four is the essential spring board for everything they do as they grow.

That's one of the reasons why it's so important to establish the relationship with your child I discussed in the last section, why it's important to *be there* with them much of the time, talking and listening, playing and interacting. Because everything you do with your child from the moment they're born counts for something. All the experiences they have. The circumstances they're in. The vibes they pick up. It all *matters*.

That's a fundamental truth about children learning that parents sometimes overlook.

Some parents think that all learning takes place in schools between the ages of four and sixteen. It doesn't. Some parents think teaching is required for learning to take place. It isn't. It starts at home through your interaction. That's why whatever you do with them matters.

But don't think of it in educational or school terms or you'll spoil it. Just make times to engage with them, to observe the world together, to discuss it, to encourage an interest in it and how everything works, and stimulate their curiosity.

Children are naturally curious about everything. Their curiosity is one of *the most valuable* starting points for them to learn about things. If we can keep their curiosity in the things around them alive, their desire to learn will stay alive, and it's that *desire to learn* that educates them and which affects their education throughout their life.

Children who are curious are bound to want to find out, to know, to explore and discover. To learn. And even though you might think this is wearing sometimes, it's extremely positive; it means your child is developing his knowledge, intelligence and his skills all the time. And he's *motivated* to learn – the lack of which can be an enormous stumbling block to education in later life.

These natural opportunities stimulate learning of valuable skills all of which your child needs to develop educationally and, more important, personally. Skills and knowledge are the basis from which every child goes forward to find and live a fulfilled and productive life.

That's why your attention to them in small everyday ways matters so much. *Your attention educates.*

And *you* need to pay the world attention too. Your interest, your interest in the world at large, in finding things out too, also has another impact. It demonstrates a positive attitude to learning. And that affects how well they learn. Both now and, importantly, later in life too.

Through the attitude you show towards learning things they will develop their own attitude towards learning things. So whether they engage with it, or think learning is worth bothering with, will be a reflection of whether you show you like to learn and think it's worth bothering with.

That's why it matters that you make your attitude to things around you one of interest and curiosity. Your attitude shows them that learning is worth it. Learning matters.

Your attitude can show that learning is exciting – even if it's just learning how to stack beakers and watching the tower fall. It can show that learning is fascinating and has an impact – like learning how to manipulate scissors. That learning is such fun – looking at a book about dinosaurs together. That learning helps us grow – like playing a computer game and gaining skills that help us progress through the levels. That learning helps us – like learning how to do up buttons. That learning makes us feel fulfilled – like learning how to make muffins!

All these simple everyday things you show an interest in helps your child learn about his world and plays a vital role in the development of his personal education.

Learn about things together. Promote learning as worthwhile, whatever it is you're learning about.

Some of the best ways to develop your child's capacity to learn are the simplest. Here are a few:

Through conversations; talking together, back and forth, about whatever you're doing is an opportunity to tell them so much. And more importantly it promotes language and communication skills, it makes them articulate, it develops vocabulary and thinking skills to name a few. Chat about what you're doing or what you're both going to do together and why. Explain why things are happening. Answer their why questions. Use your conversations for observation and questioning.

Making observations and posing questions; this can be easily included in your chatter. Observe what you see, point things out, bring your child's attention to things. Like saying; 'look at that tiny little ant.' 'I wonder what sort of flower that is?' 'Now what do we need to buy today?' 'What a huge lorry.' This kind of chatter stimulates your child's mind and that valuable curiosity about the world. Observe what people are doing and discuss why. Encourage them to ask their own questions.

Reading to them; not trying to teach them to read – just enjoying stories or non-fiction together in whatever format. Reading to them is the basis for them reading for themselves. Reading for themselves is founded in a love of stories, books and eBooks. Any time spent together enjoying books and stories in whatever format is valuable. Reading to them encourages interest in language, shows how it works, demonstrates the skills needed. It is one of the most valuable things you could be doing with your children – whatever age.

Play; it's the foundation of a multitude of skills. Many parents don't get how educative play is. But practical play is one of the most educative activities a child can be doing. Through play children learn about the things around them. For example they learn about the properties of things – hard, soft, liquid, solid, etc, they learn how to use things and gain hand-eye coordination skills – how scissors cut or paper folds, jugs fill and pour, things stack, etc, they gain practical skills – climbing, running, catching balls, etc. So many basic skills increase through play. Practical play is the best, play where they're engaged using tools and materials, recycled junk, art and craft materials, pots and pans, constructional or collectable toys, toys that stimulate them to do things rather than just passively watch a screen or play a computer game. They don't need complicated, expensive equipment – a den under the kitchen table made with an old sheet or a collection of old boxes stimulates their imagination just as much. Imagination promotes intelligent thinking. Thinking skills are essential to learning.

Through engaging them in the things you do; shopping, cooking, mending things, recycling, going places, whatever you're doing is an opportunity to engage them, talk to them, explain, involve. It may sometimes need to be on their level, i.e. if you're cooking give them some of their own 'ingredients' to play-cook with or wash plastic pots at the sink, or an old item to dismantle. But if they are involved in life they learn about life.

Physical activity is another educative activity that parents sometimes overlook. You both should be engaging in regular physical exercise anyway whether it's walking to the shops or a play in the park and spending time outdoors. But apart from keeping fit physical activity also stimulates mental activity. Mental activity is what's required for learning and education. Physical activity is good for your child in so many ways; it promotes self confidence, health – mental as well as physical, relaxation and sleep, makes them feel happier, helps with development – including that of the brain, increases general wellbeing.

So, in conclusion, just remember that everything you do with your child from the moment they are born, not only will build you a strong relationship, it will count towards their education too. And your child's attitude towards their world as being something worth learning about will rub off on others. So through your attention you bestow enormous benefits not only on your child and your relationships but, via their interaction, on the wider world too.

As a mum, is there anything you could be doing more worthwhile than that!

                                                End

Printed in Great Britain
by Amazon.co.uk, Ltd.,
Marston Gate.